# Four Fingers and Thirteen Toes

Rosaleen Moriarty-Simmonds

authorHOUSE®

AuthorHouse™ UK Ltd.
500 Avebury Boulevard
Central Milton Keynes, MK9 2BE
www.authorhouse.co.uk
Phone: 08001974150

First published – 2007

Published by AuthorHouse 29/1/2009

ISBN: 978-1-4389-4299-5 (sc)


Printed in the United States of America
Bloomington, Indiana

This book is printed on acid-free paper.

All enquiries to:
22 Cyncoed Avenue,
Cyncoed,
CARDIFF. CF23 6SU.
United Kingdom.

Email: rms-bookorders@dsl.pipex.com

# DEDICATION

In memory of my beloved mother, Ellen Philomena
(Mena) Moriarty, who through her love, devotion
and encouragement gave me the strength,
courage and conviction to be who I am today.

# Acknowledgements

The author would like to extend thanks to the following, who have helped and assisted in this publication:

Tim Richards, journalist and broadcaster, for his introduction to the book;
The staff at the Thalidomide Trust for their assistance in providing statistical and historical information;
Rebecca Sleeman for her help in designing the book cover;
To Mark Cleghorn of Mark Cleghorn Photography, Cardiff, for portrait photography;
All my Thalidomide impaired friends;
The countless persons who have generously provided information and images on the Internet;
To my family for all the stories and anecdotes that, I hope, make the book readable and enjoyable;

And finally, to Stephen and James for being so patient with me, and without whose support I could not have completed this task. I am so proud of you both, and love you "More than this much!"

# Contents

# Introduction

Thalidomide was one of the 'horror' words of the twentieth century. Along with Auschwitz, Aberfan and Chernobyl... the very word Thalidomide still makes me shudder all these years later. It slaps me round the head with painful images of newborn babies without arms or legs. Just as mankind had been unspeakably evil in Nazi concentration camps or totally incompetent allowing a mountain of coal waste to destroy a Welsh school – so for my generation of journalists working in the late twentieth century – Thalidomide came to mean the cynical and callous cover-up of thousands of deformed births worldwide.

But that is simply the cruel 'public' face of Thalidomide, a drug supposedly developed, amongst other things, to ease women through their pregnancies in the early 1960s.

Thalidomide became something much more personal for me in 1972 when I met a cute and confident little girl named Rosie Moriarty for a feature series I wanted to write for the *Western Mail*. From those first face-to- face interviews, and through several later meetings for BBC Radio Wales documentaries, I was able to watch a woman develop

– who though she had no arms or legs – against all odds pushed herself through university in Cardiff and on to a professional career that has left non-disabled contemporaries trailing in her wake.

This story of Rosie's isn't just about Thalidomide – however cruel the physical results of that drug were. Rosie's story is about guts and determination and intelligence and skill. It's one hell of an example to all of us!

Tim Richards

Journalist and Broadcaster

# Four Fingers and Thirteen Toes

# 1.

# The Arrival of James

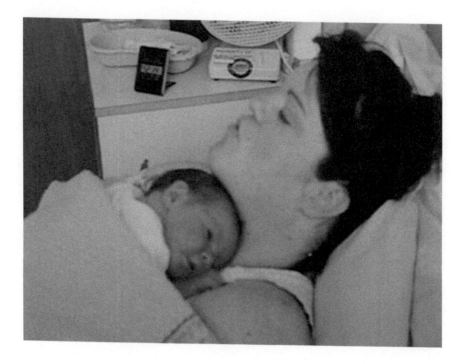

*James - two days old having a quiet cuddle with Mum*

Hello, James, my beautiful little boy," I mumbled, still drowsy from the anaesthetic. The hospital staff had brought him to me, swaddled up, with only his face showing. All I could see was a little pink face and a pair of blue eyes looking back at me. I glanced anxiously at the nurse holding him. She smiled and nodded reassuringly and I blanked out again, but with a feeling of relief.

It had not been a pleasant experience, and, had anyone bothered to ask me, I could have given them my opinion of the wonder of childbirth, an opinion that might have disillusioned many prospective mothers.

My consultant in the performance had been a strong advocate of natural childbirth, but, as he wasn't actually giving birth, I felt that he was perhaps not viewing the situation from the correct perspective. I quite fancied the idea of being knocked out and then later handed a nice, clean, pink baby; he had other ideas.

After some thirty-seven hours of the joys of labour, not much had happened, and I was becoming increasingly distressed and worried for my baby. The doctors then decided to do what should have been done in the first place. I was to have an emergency caesarean.

Until then there had been a happy air of expectancy among the staff, who were taking as keen an interest as I in the proceedings, but the arrival of the anaesthetist soon soured the mood. He refused to make eye contact with me and stood mumbling with his back to the window. He was supposed to be explaining the procedure he was about to perform, but, what with his mumbling, the lack of eye contact and the surrounding noise of the hospital, I understood nothing.

"Could you come and stand at the foot of the bed where I can see you and hear you?" I asked. "Mumble, mumble," he continued, causing my husband Stephen to explode.

The anaesthetist's attempts to give me an epidural were on par with his skills at communication and, after numerous failed attempts, the other doctors called in a senior anaesthetist, who, after a bit of prodding and poking, managed to get the drip inserted in my neck.

James was born at 8.42 p.m. on Thursday, 10 August 1995, weighing 7 pounds 2 ounces, a healthy, hearty baby eager to get on with the business of life.

The next day I was back in the regular ward, and James was in the little see-through plastic cot alongside my bed looking out at me and at the brave new world he had just entered. I looked back at him in wonderment. He was absolutely gorgeous and fascinating, and the love I felt for him was instant and intense. That warm glow of pride, love and devotion that only a mother can feel was mixed with a ferocious desire to protect, nurture and cherish. Nature and instinct are incredible things, and this normally wriggly little bundle of fun relaxed instantly whenever he was placed on me for a cuddle or when I held or carried him.

Six days later we arrived home to a house full of flowers, cards and good wishes from family, friends and acquaintances.

I doubt that there were three happier people in the whole world than Stephen, James and me. And then our joy was shared, if not quite so personally, by everyone that had known us through my pregnancy.

"So what's so wonderful about all this?" you say. "Lots of women have babies."

But I was born with legs that ended above the knee and with no arms, just two fingers on each shoulder. Four fingers and thirteen toes in all.

It does make a difference.

# 2.

# The Alchemists of Stolberg

*Otto Ambrose, one of Grünenthal's directors in the early 1950s also a chemist and a director of IG Farben.*

*Dr Heinrich Mückter was the chemist in charge of the research at Chemie Grünenthal.*

Most people, when thinking of the Ruhr Valley in Germany, have a mental picture of heavy industry, steel works and smoking chimneys, an image which is not too far from the truth. And metal has been worked here since the seventeenth century, when copper was smelted and became the prime industry of the region. As with similar industry in Britain, the Ruhr had a nearby source of coal and became the heart of Germany's industrial revolution in consequence.

Never far away from the smelters of metal were the alchemists, still seeking the secret of converting base metal into gold, a search that even the venerable Isaac Newton subscribed to, although he discreetly kept his interest secret, and their successors became the foundation of the chemical industry of the Ruhr.

Five miles to the east of the town of Aachen lies the smaller town of Stolberg, formerly a major centre for the production of copper and brass. Now its principal industry is the production of chemicals. One of its many family-owned companies is that of Chemie Grünenthal, a small manufacturer of pharmaceuticals. All pharmaceutical companies, rather in the manner of the old alchemists, if no longer searching for the touchstone to transmute base metals, were, however, searching for drugs that they could sell to the medical professions of the world. In 1953 Chemie Grünenthal were searching for antibiotics, or, more accurately, for a method of producing antibiotics cheaply from readily available peptides. Antibiotics were relatively expensive to produce, and the chemists at Grünenthal were hopeful of making a breakthrough.

A Dr Heinrich Mückter had succeeded in developing a substance that the company felt might be the answer, and the laboratory went ahead to find a way of producing it commercially.

Heating up some samples of a substance with a tongue-twisting name, phthaloyliso-glutamine, the heads of the research department, Dr W. Kunz and Dr H. Keller, produced a slightly different substance, alpha-phthalimido-glutarimide, which, although not an antibiotic as they had hoped, looked promising as a possible painkiller. Not very sure of what they had, the chemists patented it anyway and went looking for a use for the product.

Relatively small, the laboratory lacked the exhaustive testing facilities of the major pharmaceutical companies, but the chemists found that the limited tests of alpha-phthalimido-glutarimide they did carry out on animals produced no adverse results, regardless of the dosage, although the substance seemed to have little in the way of the sedative and tranquilising effects they had expected. There were no apparent side effects, so here, Chemie Grünenthal felt, would be a safe and non-lethal tranquiliser for the mass market. To market the drug, they had to prove that it was indeed a sedative as claimed. In order to prove this to the German authorities, the company set up an outrageously unscientific demonstration. Prudence would have dictated that some controlled testing of the drug be conducted before placing it on the open market, but prudence does not seem to have come into the thinking of the Grünenthal chemists.

Perhaps significantly, Otto Ambros, one of Grünenthal's Directors in the early 1950s, was also a chemist and a Director of IG Farben, a company which supplied gasoline and rubber for Hitler's war effort. He was also responsible for the choice of location, planning, building and running of IG Farben, Auschwitz.

Further, Dr Heinrich Mückter, the chemist in charge of research at Chemie Grünenthal, had been a medical officer during the Nazi occupation of Poland. He had been a member of the Wehrmachtsbetreuungskompanie 14 in Grodno from spring 1942 to December 1942. Although there is no direct evidence that he was a party to any of the medical experiments conducted frequently under the regime, questioned later in 1968, he confirmed that the Jewish workforce had been used in the facilities to fight lice, but he could not give any information about their subsequent fate or whereabouts. He did not know of any transports out of the ghettos in Grodno or even of any killing activities against the Jewish population. Under no circumstance was he eyewitness to any such activities, he claimed.

The good doctor appears to have had a selective or faulty memory, for he failed to recall the names of any of the Gestapo officers under whom he would have been working. The names Wiese, Errellis, Streblow and Schott he could not remember, and they did not ring a bell in connection with the Jews of Grodno. Yet these were the men in charge during that period when the first executions were taking place in the ghetto.

The horrific conditions in the ghetto – overcrowding, inhuman living quarters, nonexistent sanitation, serious food shortages, bitter cold and unspeakable filth – were most conducive to illness and epidemics and must surely have merited his attention.

On 2 November 1942, Ghettos 1 and 2 in Grodno were completely sealed off. In the morning the workers from Ghetto 2 were held up at the gate, and suddenly the commandants of the two ghettos, Kurt Wiese (Ghetto 1) and Otto Streblow (Ghetto 2), appeared and began shooting at the workers indiscriminately. Twelve Jews were killed, forty were wounded and the others fled wildly in panic. It was the first time that Grodno's Jews had experienced sudden mass murder, perpetrated without warning.

The sealing of the two ghettos was accompanied by show hangings and acts of group murder. The first hanging took place in the first half of November 1942. The victims were Lena Prenska (the daughter of a well- known tailor) and a refugee from Warsaw named Drucker – both had been caught on the Aryan side of the city – and Moshe Spindler, the superintendent of the apartment building in which Lena resided, for not reporting her absence. The three were taken to a central site in the ghetto and hanged in front of the Judenrat and other Jews who were ordered to watch the "spectacle." When Aharon Rubinczik, the head of the Jewish Police, balked at tying the noose around the victims' necks, Wiese did it himself. The bodies were left on the gallows until the next day as a warning to potential offenders.

This first hanging was widely publicised, and publicexecutions continued until the ghetto's liquidation the following year, yet Dr Mückter failed to recall any of these events.

A similar forgetfulness seemed to occur when he became in charge of the research laboratory at Grünenthal.

Crucially, they had failed to test the drug on pregnant females during their testing of animals, and it never seems to have occurred to anyone to do so later, when it was being promoted as being safe for expectant mothers. Even though German regulations concerning new drugs were in place to ensure that unapproved medication would not be available, the company cheerfully ignored these. No clinical trials had been completed, and no application had been made for approval of the drug other than to have it classified as a sedative.

Without carrying out any further tests, Grünenthal began to give out free samples to doctors in Switzerland and West Germany, recommending it for the control of seizures in patients with epilepsy. It appeared to work well, many patients reporting that it had a calming and soothing effect with little or no side effects, justifying the hopeful claims that it was a useful sedative. It seemed that the company had hit upon a winning formula. "Even a determined suicide could not take enough to cause death. Accidental overdoses by children would be unheard of with this drug," claimed the company.

An employee of the company took a sample home for his pregnant wife who was suffering from severe morning sickness. It cured her sickness, but on Christmas Day 1956, his child was born – without ears.

It seems not to have registered in the minds of the chemists, for ten months later the drug went on sale over the counter in Germany as the drug of choice for pregnant women. Although the label contained the name *phthalimido-glutarimide* in very small letters, the company's marketing department realised that they would have to come up with a more commercial name if it was to become a big seller.

They named it *'Thalidomide.'*

A year beforehand an Irish family, Mr and Mrs James Cummins and their daughter Mena, more formally christened Ellen Philomena, had landed in Cardiff to start a new life. Little did they know how much the chemists, so busily working away in far off Stolberg, were going to affect their lives.

# 3.

# Destination Cardiff

*Dad as a young single man during his early years in Cardiff.*

*Mum on her confirmation day in her early teens,*
*before the family's moving to Cardiff.*

W onderful," exclaimed Papa Cummins, surveying the outlook of the city before him on a sunny day in September 1956. "Always was fond of Cardiff. When I was in the merchant navy, we used to dock right down there," he waved his hand vaguely in the direction of the port, "And I used to say that if there were any place in the world other than Ireland that I'd live, it would be here. And now, here we all are," he concluded, triumphantly. His wife and daughter saw no reason to contradict him, for the town did have a pleasant look with the summer sunlight playing on the stone of the buildings. Much of the town was constructed from a local stone, a yellowish lias limestone, not unlike that of Portland, giving it a cheerfully sunny look even on the dullest of days. It was a far cry from the little fishing village of Ballyhack, just outside of Waterford in Wexford County, where Papa had been a fisherman and they had all grown up.

In 1956 Cardiff was no longer the major port that it had been around the turn of the century, but, compared with the job prospects in Ireland at the time, it had become something of a Mecca for Irish seeking employment. And now my grandfather, grandmother and my soon-to-be mother, now fourteen years old and today celebrating her birthday, had arrived on the doorstep of the city that only the previous year had become the capital of Wales.

They were following in the steps of many before them. In fact, the rather unique accent of the people of Cardiff, distinctively different from the usual Welsh of the surrounding villages, was attributed to the influx of the Irish around the turn of the century when it was Britain's busiest port. They had brought much-needed labour to the region, and – as is the way in such matters – the locals had eventually come to resent it. Prejudice is endemic in human nature. I doubt whether there is anyone on this earth who is not prejudiced in some way about something. In the case of the landladies of Cardiff, whilst they may have had a few unique prejudices of their own, in general they stuck to just two. Almost every lodging house hanging the notice 'accommodation' in its front window had appended a corollary – 'No Blacks, No Irish'.

Papa and Nana and, of course, my mother spent some anxious hours plodding the streets of the city in search of a place to settle. His enthusiasm for the town remained undimmed in spite of this minor setback and was fully justified when they hit on just the spot. The landlady proved to be Irish.

The search for work proved easier than they had ever imagined, and, with the help of their landlady, both found work at the Cardiff Royal Infirmary. Nana became a housekeeper, looking after the nurses and Papa a porter in the hospital. In those days the school leaving age was fourteen, and Mum quickly found a job as a junior, very junior, shop assistant in Thayer's ice cream store in the Roath area of the City.

Industrious and friendly, they soon integrated themselves into the local community, and Mum was starting to grow up fast. Working in a busy store gave her an entree into the social life of the town, and she proved herself a popular and hard-working employee with a great sense of humour. Life was indeed looking good for the whole family.

In the following year, a young man by the name of Denis Moriarty set out from Ardfert, a small town not far from Tralee, to join his older brother, Tom, already well established in Cardiff. Seventeen years old, he had come to Cardiff to complete an engineering apprenticeship. Back home, like so many others, he felt that there were more opportunities to be had abroad. The boom times that were later to come to Ireland seemed pretty remote to any ambitious young man at that time, especially when viewed from places such as Ardfert, where scope was decidedly limited.

And he was ambitious. Almost as soon as his feet had touched the streets of Cardiff, he was on the lookout for opportunities. His first job was with a small engineering company in Newport, a few miles down the road from Cardiff, and at once his ability and enthusiasm were noted. Ever impatient, he saw that working for himself would be his future. As time went on, he started working two other jobs besides, saving the money to buy a truck with which to go into business for himself as a private contractor. At that time there was a tremendous amount of new construction going on around Cardiff, and trucks and drivers were in great demand. Coal was still being exported from the docks, and the huge steel mill nearby was a major employer and consumer of local services.

It would be two years before the paths of the two families would cross; meanwhile, the alchemists of Stolberg had not been idle.

# The Great Cardiff Poem

**C**ars, trains, traffic jams

**A**erial views, castles, shops and dams

**R**eally groovy places to go

**D**isabled people must go with the flow

**I**n-house theatres, sport and culture

**F**amily atmosphere, gazing in wonder

**F**un, sexy, wise and cool

**Cardiff is happening – open your eyes, you fool!**

By

Rosaleen Moriarty-Simmonds

2002

# 4.

# Hard Selling

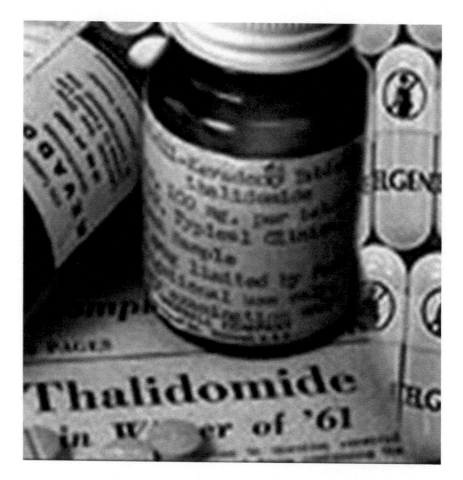

*Thalidomide tablets (bottled) from the 1960s side
by side with Thalidomide capsules of today.*

The success reported by the doctors who had received their free samples of the drug, prompted Grünenthal to go ahead with their plans for marketing it as an over-the-counter remedy for a number of conditions but primarily as a tranquiliser and painkiller, one with no undesirable side effects. Almost like one of the patent medicines beloved of the Victorians, it was even touted as a cough, cold and flu remedy, a cure for all ills. They seem to have disregarded the few unfavourable comments of side effects (i.e. nerve damage in patients using the drug for prolonged periods) they had received from the doctors who had made use of the free samples and continued to tout it as a drug completely free from all undesirable consequences, one that could be taken almost regardless of dosage with safety. For the general public, the name of Contergan was chosen initially, just one of the bewildering number of names – some fifty-one were registered eventually – used for the product as it went on sale worldwide in forty-six countries, eleven of them in Europe alone. Only in the United States did they fail to introduce the drug initially. The reason for this will be explained later. Incredibly, not one of the countries in which the drug was marketed seemed to have questioned its safety, apparently taking Grünenthal's sales pitch that, "This powerful hypnotic drug is completely safe," at face value.

In Britain the product was launched by the Distillers Company (Biochemicals) Limited in April 1958, where the names Distaval, Tensival, Asmaval, Valgis and Valgraine were used in addition to Thalidomide, and the companies were now recommending the product specifically for pregnant women. Promoted as a *"wonder drug"* to combat morning sickness, the literature that accompanied it stressed that it could be used "Without any risk to mother or child". The literature also said, "Side effects are virtually absent" and "The answer to the mounting deaths due to barbiturate poisoning" were also part of the sales pitch. Distiller's Development Manager R. Gresham tried to sound a note of caution, saying that he felt that the phrase "No known toxicity" was, in his words, "Rather sweeping." He suggested that "Exceptionally low toxicity" would have been more appropriate. Little did he suspect just how toxic the drug was to prove to be.

Some unsung bureaucrats in the British Government rubber-stamped their approval to manufacture, based solely on the claims of Grünenthal.

By March 1961 nearly 64 million tablets had been sold in Britain, and the accompanying literature told doctors that "Distaval can be given with complete safety to pregnant women and nursing mothers without adverse effect on mother or child." The doctors had no reason to doubt the claims; after all, the drug had been approved by the government. And still the product remained virtually untested, un-approved and, in Germany anyway, available across the counter to all and sundry. Distillers not only made no serious attempts to test the drug themselves but also failed to question the data provided by the laboratory.

Distillers did run a few cursory tests on the drug but tended to ignore any negative results. Two months before it went on sale, one of the men who had conducted the tests wrote in *The British Medical Journal,* "It would seem unjustifiable to use the drug for long term sedative or hypnotic therapy, pending the results of more detailed study of its long term effects in a larger series of patients, notably those suffering from mild or moderately severe hyperthyroidism."

The cautionary note was overlooked, and the drug went on sale.

Grünenthal, for their part, were conducting an aggressive sales campaign, with 50 advertisements in major medical journals, 200,000 letters to doctors around the world and 50,000 leaflets to pharmacists. By the end of the first year, sales had reached 90,000 packets per month worldwide.

But questions were already being raised, although the matter of deformed births had not yet reared its head. Most were related to perceived neurological problems in recipients of the drug. Questioned, Grünenthal responded, "Happily, we can tell you that such disadvantageous effects have not been brought to our notice."

But it was not true. There were plenty of warning signs.

The company responded by mailing out 250,000 copies of a new brochure in 1960, ignoring all the warnings and repeating the claims of non-toxicity. But the sales department seemed to have been more aware of the problems than were the laboratory technicians:

"Unfortunately, we are now receiving increasingly strong reports on the side effects of thalidomide, as well as letters from doctors and pharmacists who want to put it on prescription. From our side, everything must be done to avoid this since a substantial amount of our volume comes from over the counter sales."

And still the true horror of the effects of the drug had not made themselves known.

In spite of their public posturing, internally Grünenthal must have been well aware that the golden goose that they thought they had, was laying an addled egg. At a staff meeting in July 1961, Grünenthal's staff doctor admitted, "If I were a doctor (GP), I would not prescribe Contergan any more."

But the genie had escaped from the bottle. The drug was available worldwide across the counter.

Not until it was too late, in 1961, did a researcher from the U.S. Food and Drug Administration reveal the shoddy research that had gone into the product, by which time it had already entered the market there, although only on a trial basis, awaiting certification.

The mechanism for testing that had been used by the manufacturer, was accurately described later as one of *Russian Roulette*, only this time the game was to be played with the lives of unborn children. Before the end of 1961 – 2 December 1961 – to be precise, when Grünenthal reluctantly pulled the drug off the market, enough had been distributed to cause 8,000 children to have been born with defects in forty-six countries. Some estimates put the number of stillbirths at twice that number. And many survived for only a few years. We now know that these figures were grossly underestimated.

# 5.

# The Shadow of Stolberg

*Mum and Dad on their wedding day.*

*L-R: Tom (Dad's eldest brother), Dad, Mum, Bridget
(Tom's wife), Nana and Papa Cummins.*

It was, I suppose, almost inevitable in the fairly confined social milieu of the Irish population in Cardiff, that my mother and father should meet. More remarkable, given that it was a tight-knit community, was the fact that they met on a blind date, not having known each other previously. I imagine that the success rates of such encounters are pretty low, but in this case it was to be a memorable exception to the rule. But then again, the date had been set up by Tom and Bridget; later to become my Godparents.

He was nineteen. Handsome enough, but that alone would not have been sufficient for my mother. She found him to be a perfect match for her own personality, and the feeling was mutual.

In her he found an admirable foil to his rather more introverted personality, and her sense of humour lit up both their lives. Almost without saying there was little doubt that they would be together, and so on 4 June 1960 they were wed in the Catholic Church of St Peters near the City Centre with the full blessing of their families.

Those of you with a mathematical bent will soon spot that there was, for the period, a rather short time between their marriage and my birth in December of the same year, and it was quite remarkable under the circumstances that there seems to have been no undue stigma as a result. Both families, it seemed, were unfazed by what would have been regarded at the time as something to be hushed up. But then, my father was very handsome and my mother very attractive. It seemed that nothing could possibly mar their happiness. And her pregnancy would seem to put a seal upon it rather than a burden. Impending motherhood made her more radiant than ever. The only regrettable factor was that accursed morning sickness which plagued her.

It was then that her doctor prescribed a newly developed treatment to help her. Thalidomide was totally harmless, she was told, a new wonder drug being distributed by one of Britain's most respected drug companies. Miraculously, the pills did the trick. However, later in the pregnancy she developed a case of toxaemia. She was admitted into hospital for a month or so, to prevent anything untoward occurring during the pregnancy. In those days, there was no pregnancy scanning to determine if the baby was in good shape or not; it was a matter of chance.

On 6 December 1960, I was born in the Glossop Maternity Hospital, Cardiff. My mother was eighteen years old, my father only twenty, and nothing had prepared them for the events that followed. The midwife took one horrified look and snatched me away from my mother. There was much frantic muttering, and then they gave my mother a powerful sedative. She thought I must have been born dead.

But I was very much alive and blissfully unaware of the problems I was causing, not least to the hospital staff who were traumatised by my appearance.

Worse was to follow, for when my father arrived at the hospital unaware of the crisis, not a soul could bring themselves to tell him that I had no arms and that my legs, truncated above the knee, were doubled up over my abdomen. Finally, a senior doctor was called from the main hospital to perform the impossible task of explaining matters to my father, matters which he himself could not comprehend. For hours he walked my poor father around. What he said I have no idea, and I doubt that he could recall either, until finally dad was persuaded to go home and rest.

But there, at my grandparents', they were eagerly awaiting news. Was it a boy or a girl? Grief stricken, my father was inconsolable and had to be restrained by my grandparents from injuring himself. I can only imagine the scene. How they got through the next few days I have no idea.

Back at the hospital, they were keeping my mother sedated, no doubt wondering how on earth to handle the matter. But by then she must have realised that her baby had not been stillborn. Ripping out the sedation drip from her arm, she tried to make her way to the nursery but collapsed before she could get anywhere near. Wisely, the doctors saw that the best thing to do was to let her see me.

I was brought to her, wrapped up like a mummy with only my face showing. She held me very tightly and then, slowly and deliberately, undid the wrappings. She looked calmly at my little body and said, "Isn't she beautiful? She's all mine."

We fell instantly in love from that moment, a love that has never wavered. And she was barely eighteen years old at the time.

Of course, there was I, quietly contented and not realising what a kerfuffle I was causing in the adult world. Also, at the time, I did not realise how incredibly lucky I was to have such wonderful parents, nor, for that matter, what a superbly supportive family group

I had been born into. For, in spite of everything, I was accepted without the slightest demur. I was Rosie, their much loved and protected daughter, and nothing else mattered. I was to come home to them.

But society doesn't always see it that way. It abhors the different and has trouble accepting that not everybody may have the normal complement of bits and pieces that they find acceptable. Working on this premise, my parents were counselled by the doctors. "Look here," they said, "You're both young; you have all your lives before you. Why don't you just leave her here at the hospital with us? Go away and start life anew."

They were horrified. Such a thing flew not only in the face of their religion but also, and more important, in the face of their feelings. I went home with them, into the home of my grandparents.

And it was the luckiest day of my life.

# 6.

# Starting Out

*Me and my Dad, my first birthday at St Mary's Hospital, Paddington, London.*

*Mum and I (aged 2 years old) during yet another hospital stay.*

I can only imagine the events of the first few weeks of my life. I was undoubtedly cosseted, cuddled and probably shielded from the outside world. None of my physical failings would have been of any importance to me at that stage, and, once the initial trauma had subsided, my parents would have behaved in much the same way that parents do with their first born. But it was not going to be easy for them.

Within our family group, there was no problem. It was with the rest of the world that the difficulties presented themselves. Mum and Dad were under constant pressure from both doctors and priests (who, in my opinion, should have known better) to put me in an institution. Some 45 per cent of Thalidomide children found themselves dumped, deserted or forsaken. Basically, unwanted and unloved in institutions such as Chailey Heritage School in East Sussex, to be brought up by the nurses or carers. No doubt cared for well enough in their way, but nothing to compare with the love of a family.

So great was the pressure from these undoubtedly well-meaning folks that Mum and Dad actually got as far as taking me to the gates of Nazareth House in Cardiff to be adopted. Originally founded in the 1870s as the Convent of Poor Sisters of Nazareth, the orphanage was now housed in the rather splendid Nazareth House that had been designed by John Prichard and built in around 1847 for the third Marquis of Bute. Standing outside this palatial, gloomy building, they paused, and without even saying a word to each other, turned and took me back home. Had I been old enough, I would have breathed a sigh of relief, for, without that family background,

I would never have succeeded in making my life as full as it is today. My parents were the reason for my survival and success.

Sometimes their agony must have been almost unbearable. Later my mother told me of the first time that she had taken me out shopping with her. A woman, looking into the pram said, "Oh, what a beautiful baby." Then, pulling back the covers a little, she saw my little stumpy arms with two fingers sprouting from each shoulder.

She screamed, "My God, it's a freak," and went running up the road as though afraid that I might be contagious. My mother, not surprisingly, was devastated and heartbroken. For a while it put her off taking me out in public, but her logical reasoning – and she was a very logical and pragmatic person – led her to understand that it was the ignorance of others and that such situations were neither her fault nor my fault. But it was difficult for her forget, and probably to forgive.

The attentions of the medical profession were another hurdle to be overcome. On seeing an imperfect body, their instinct was to do something to make it conform more or less to the norm. Whether this would improve matters or not, did not seem to be of much account. "Here is a piece of damaged goods," they would say. "Let us do what we can to make it look like all the rest of us."

And so they got to work on me at St Mary's Hospital in Paddington, London, a location that meant that I was to be separated from my family for long periods, as they could only afford to visit from time to time.

When archaeologists dig up a damaged piece of statuary, they resist the temptation to replace the missing bits, leaving it as the work of art that it was when they found it. Doctors do not see it that way. From a personal point of view, it would have been more comfortable had I been found by an archaeologist.

Their first efforts were dedicated to straightening my little legs, using all sorts of metal contraptions with pins through my bones and bolts being tightened every day to stretch my reluctant limbs. Torquemada had nothing on these people.

And so my first birthday was *celebrated*, if that's the right word, in hospital but at any rate with a visit from all my family, who came en masse from Cardiff laden with presents. The nurses and staff joined in too, and, although I can't recall much in the way of detail, I still have memories and images in my mind of the nurses in their grey uniforms and of that smell, the smell of hospitals, an amalgam of blood, bleach, wee, poo, starch, rubber gloves all disguised, unsatisfactorily, by a heavy overtone of Dettol disinfectant.

Kind as they all were, without my parents I was lonely and sad, crying for no reason other than the emptiness of life without them. An old Cockney couple came and visited me regularly. They were friends of the hospital, and brought a small measure of welcome sunlight into my life.

But Christmas came and, joy of joys, I was to go home for the holiday.

The weather was atrocious. It had been snowing for days, and people were advised not to travel. My wonderful parents, determined as ever, were not going to leave me in hospital over Christmas. They struggled for hours through roads and lanes with snow that had been piled almost as high as houses. Exhausted and cold, unable to get any further because of the snow blockages, they stopped at a roadside café. It was full of lorry drivers, truckers and salesmen who had given up on their journeys for sanctuary in the café. They thought that Mum and Dad, mere youngsters at the time, were mad to have even attempted the journey. When they explained the reasons for doing so, a quiet voice came from the corner of the café and said, "In that case you had better follow me." It turned out that he had a snowplough, and he cleared the path for them through lanes and roads all the way to the hospital, just so that a little girl could go home for Christmas.

It was apparently an epic trip across a snowbound country, but when one is just one year old and a little bit, you take this sort of thing in your stride. I was just happy to be back home.

What I could not take in my stride, however, were the needles, the anaesthetics, the blood samples and the series of operations that medical science felt were necessary. To this day I cannot stand needles or having my face and nose covered. It is too reminiscent of being put under for another op, and, for the next few years, operations were to fill my life.

But, fortunately, my parents were there also to fill my life with their love and affection for me, a love that was never in any doubt in spite of a seemingly thoughtless world that must often have challenged them. They had taken one piece of advice though. They had got on with their lives, as the doctors had suggested and, to their eternal credit, had included me in that life. And then there was a new addition to the family when Deborah arrived on 18 March 1962.

Dad phoned the hospital.

"Is it a boy or a girl?" he asked.

"It's a girl, Mr. Moriarty," the nurse replied.

"Has she..., err, has she got ten fingers and ten toes?"

There was a bewildered silence from the other end, before a baffled nurse, probably wondering if my father had been celebrating a little too well, responded:

"But of course. What did you expect?"

# 7.

# Realisation

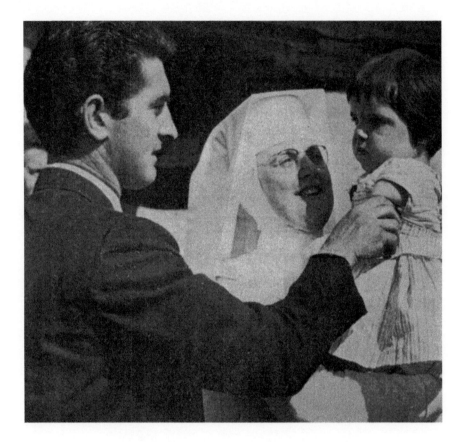

*Dad and Rosie say good-bye before the
first of many trips to Lourdes.*

My life, such as it was, seemed to revolve around doctors and specialists, medical assessments and discussions about rehabilitation. There was talk of my being fitted with artificial limbs, courtesy of The Nuffield Orthopaedic Hospital in Oxford. Naturally, I was not consulted and began to feel myself to be more of a practice dummy for the medical profession than a real person. In spite of my age, I must have been aware of the grave discussions being held over me and of the lengthy consultations with my parents, who, I suppose, could do little else but let the doctors get on with it. And, strangely, no one seemed to be interested in the why of the matter, only in attempting to remedy the error that nature seemed to have made.

But in far off Australia, an obstetrician by the name of Dr W.G. McBride was becoming interested. On 6 November 1961, shortly before my first birthday, he had a letter published in the *Lancet* stating that babies of women who were given Thalidomide during pregnancy frequently had limb deformities of a very distinct type. Barely five months later, a letter in the same journal stated that Thalidomide given to pregnant rabbits resulted in the birth of litters in which identical effects were seen. Thus within six months of the suggested association between Thalidomide and foetal deformity, there was evidence for a striking similarity – rather than a difference – between mammalian species. It was the vital research that the men of Grünenthal had not bothered to perform.

Suddenly, there was a surge of interest in such cases, and the result was that a succession of social workers would drag their students around to 'look at an interesting case' (i.e. me).

After receiving a succession of these calls, which resulted in neither financial nor physical help, let alone any spiritual or practical support, Mum decided that the free show should end.

Thus the next social busybody that appeared on our doorstep must have been surprised when my normally placid and charming mother told her, "Sod off! And don't come back." I rather wish I had been old enough to appreciate it.

But all was not dross now that I was seen to be a victim of a serious bit of medical malfeasance. My status went from a freak of nature to that of a victim and with it, rather unreasonably in fact, there was a distinct change in attitude towards me.

By now I was appreciating something of my potential star quality and was able to enjoy a day out at a fund-raising garden party held by Lady Hoare, then the wife of the Lord Mayor of London. I was now two and one-half years old and well able to appreciate the fuss being made. Benny Hill, the TV star, kidnapped me for the day and started me off on a lifetime of interest in show business and famous people, for there were many in attendance with their children, including the Beverley Sisters.

It was a wonderful day for me and Lady Hoare, who, through her Lady Hoare Trust, became a valuable ally in the later fight for compensation for victims of Thalidomide. She saw clearly that the child being cared for in her own home would be infinitely better off than one placed in a home for disabled people and campaigned tirelessly to achieve this. Had I been asked, I would have heartily endorsed her opinion.

Both my parents were devout Catholics, and it was decided to make a pilgrimage to Lourdes. Only my mum would be travelling with me, as Dad had to work, and anyway the trip for two would have been far too expensive. I was already quite a costly proposition compared with the average child. I don't know if the trip was to be in expectation of a miracle, but I rather think it was more likely to have been a gesture of thanks for my being. It turned out that I was the youngest ever to travel from Wales, and the *Catholic Herald* ran a front-page picture of me and Dad saying goodbye before the trip! The caption read: "Three hundred Welsh pilgrims led by Archbishop Murphy of Cardiff and Bishop Petit of Menevia flew from Cardiff last week for the Welsh National Pilgrimage to Lourdes. Our picture shows three-year-old Rosaleen Moriarty saying goodbye to her father before boarding the plane. Rosaleen, who was a Thalidomide baby, was the youngest pilgrim."

Once there I was installed in a hospital room while Mum stayed at a local hotel. It was all very exciting, and I had a daily visit from the amiable Archbishop John Murphy, to whom I took a special fancy, calling him "Murf" and borrowing his dog collar, a performance he seemed to enjoy as much as I.

At the ceremony of the blessing of the sick, a solemn and sacred occasion, he stopped directly in front of me and Mum. Not appreciating the solemnity of the moment – at three years old one doesn't always understand these nuances – I called out, "Hey, Murf.

Murf. I'm down here. I see you've got your dog collar on today."

No doubt I was hastily hushed up, but I'm sure he would have been amused by it. He was that kind of a priest.

Later that year the father of a Thalidomide child, Richard Satterley, had a letter published in a London newspaper urging parents of any child who had suffered as a result of the mother using the drug Thalidomide during pregnancy to join him in suing the drug company. His son Richard had been born, as had I, with missing limbs, and he felt that there was by now enough evidence to indict the company or companies that were responsible for distributing the drug. Naturally, the company, Distillers, did not see it that way.

There was a substantial response to his appeal – sixty-two sets of parents. The costs involved with bringing up an impaired child were not inconsiderable, and, even though there had been a government-issued licence to produce the drug, the government were singularly disinterested in discussing the matter. It is often said that only fools turn to law, but for the parents there was no other remedy.

A meeting was convened in London, and Mum and Dad attended, the delegates sporting carnations so that they might be recognised. As a result, two writs were issued for our family, one on behalf of me and one for my mother. The total cost was to be £10, a not insubstantial sum for us in those days, but, as usual, the family chipped in and the writs were duly issued.

Meanwhile, I was learning to be as normal a little girl as was possible, and the doctors were busily trying to make me perfect, which, to me, meant that they were trying to make me abnormal. In spite of their efforts, I was enjoying myself, unaware of writs that were about to fly or the more and more gruesome discoveries that were being made on the subject of Thalidomide and its consequences.

All was not easy for my family, however.

We now had our own council house at 19 Heol Gwyneth in Birchgrove, Cardiff, and, most wonderful of all, neighbours who accepted me uncompromisingly. I was now mobile on a rather inconvenient set of 'rockers', stubby little artificial legs, but they did enable me to get about, and I would spend much time in the houses of our neighbours, often returning home with flowers or perhaps a cake that I had scrounged.

But the groundswell of protest over the Thalidomide scandal was growing. Now some 450 children in Britain alone had been diagnosed as having been impaired by the drug.

Distillers had something to answer for. But they remained silent. It would not be until the end of the 1960s that they would grudgingly offer some compensation for their lack of due diligence.

# 8.

# Off to School

*At Nuffield Orthopaedic Hospital, where endless
hours of rehabilitation was the order of the day,
to try to master my artificial arms and legs.*

*Much happier at home sharing a joke with the family.*

Unaware of all this commotion, I continued to play quite happily, if not comfortably, on my little rocking legs, and I doubt that many children had such a happy home life. I must have been horribly spoiled, I'm sure. I suppose I was dimly aware that I was not like all the others, the children around me, but at this age it made little difference.

What did make the difference, however, was the determined efforts of the medical profession to equip me with all sorts of mechanical paraphernalia in the misguided impression that it would improve my life. Sad to say, it did not, and the process of wiring, bolting and screwing of all these contrivances on to my body was both unpleasant and painful.

Not only that, but mastering these mechanical marvels proved to be a step too far in many cases. Solicitously, they fitted us with crash helmets, transforming us in to 'Metal Mickeys', a process that rather defeated their avowed purpose of making us less conspicuous in the world. One particularly ingenious device involved artificial arms powered by compressed gas, carried in a cylinder on your back, hardly something that could be easily concealed. There seemed to be no provision for any backup system in case the gas should run out at a critical moment when, I suppose, you would remain frozen in the last attitude adopted until help arrived with another canister.

Included in my medical records there is film footage of me struggling to manipulate these stupid arms. I suppose the doctors were so proud of their ingenious contraptions that they failed to notice that I could perform all the tasks much quicker and more easily using the resources that nature had provided me.

But all these attempts proved to be, for me, a blessing, if at the time a blessing heavily disguised, not because of the weird and wonderful bits of machinery, but because of a much more human frailty.

Although I was unaware of it then – at five years old it is not something that strikes you at the time – someone had fallen in love with me!

We had gone to the Prudential Building in the centre of Cardiff for yet another session of what was euphemistically called *'limb fitting'*. I often wonder what the guests at what is now the Hilton Hotel would think if they realised that their accommodation was at one time used for the purpose. Rather as though it had previously been a plague house, I suspect.

But there I met and became good friends with Stephen, like myself a Thalidomide baby. He had come off rather better, inasmuch as his arms were fully developed. Little did I suspect at the time that he was to be my future husband.

As children who were socially and physically different, it was inevitable that we would keep on bumping into each other on similar occasions. And sometimes the bumping was literal as we tried to master our artificial limbs.

However, I'm getting ahead of myself in my story.

I'm sure that I would have been perfectly content to have stayed at home, playing in the gully behind our house, gathering wild flowers and having tea and cakes with the neighbours, but society dictates that, just when you're getting a grip upon life, they ruin the whole thing by making you go to school.

Not too big a deal for the average kid, but, if you are, so to speak, out of the normal run of things, it became, in the years of the 1960s, a far more elaborate and unsatisfactory affair.

For in those days disabled children of the world were lumped together regardless of their impairment.

Mum and Dad wanted me to go to school with all the other local kids, which included my cousins and subsequently sister's. But it seems it was the teachers and education system who were to be obstructive, not me, by their inability to cope with something a little out of the ordinary. I had to go to a 'Special School'.

This was, of course, located as inconveniently as possible, some miles away in Penarth, requiring a taxi ride to and from home.

The school, Ysgol Erw'r Delyn, undoubtedly tried its hardest and socially provided as good an environment for us as possible. But academically it was a letdown. Not because of a lack of willingness on the part of the staff but because of the bizarre official opinion that, well, disabled was disabled. It was perceived that you were incapable of doing anything, and that was an end to it. The fact that my brain, and that of a good many others, was as sharp as any kid's with all his or her limbs never seemed to have crossed their minds. It had, however, crossed my parents' minds. My sister Debbie was now at the local school and, rather proudly, I suspect, was boasting of her elder sister who had no arms and no legs. Hearing this, the teacher gave her a sound telling off for lying and then confronted my mother and demanded to know why wasn't I at school.

But still the local authority refused to allow me the chance of a real education.

But I made friends at school. One, Beverley Rastin, with the same four-limbed *Phocomelia* (foreshortened arms and legs) as I had, became especially close, and we soon became known as "The terrible twins," no doubt with good reason. She was fair and slim whilst I was dark and round – some combination!

If academically a bit on the skimpy side, I thoroughly enjoyed the social aspect, where the two high spots of the year would be our Christmas play and sports day. Then the ham in me would come to the fore. I still remember the last school play I was in which starred myself and Keith Jenkins, known as 'Beefy'. As we had also written it together, no doubt I gave myself a pretty good part alongside my co-star, probably nicknamed 'Beefy' with good reason although I can't remember clearly why!

As for the sports days, the teachers had to use their imagination and a lot of lateral thinking to come up with games that people of vastly differing abilities could all take part in. So, apart from the running races, shot put, javelin and others, there were wheelchair races, clock golf and donut-eating competitions. The latter being my favourite. The ring donuts were hanging from a pole on various lengths of string, and participants had to eat as many as possible in three minutes with their hands behind their backs. This made it fairer for people like me who either didn't have any, or had limited arm movement.

And all these pleasant happenings were interspersed with more and more unpleasant visits to hospitals and clinics, sometimes as far afield as to the Nuffield Orthopaedic Hospital in Oxford. More expense, more unpleasant attempts to mould me into something that I was never meant to be and more frustration when all the ingenious devices did nothing for me.

# 9.

# Coping

*Being OK about my appearance, even if the*
*bunches do make me stand out!*

Our family increased in May 1967 with the arrival of another sister, Denise. As the hospital would not allow us in to see our new addition, Debbie and I were taken to the hospital to view this miracle from the grounds through the window. It was pouring with rain, and then we saw Mum holding up a howling pink bundle at the window. We looked in horror at this apparition that was apparently being foisted upon our family.

But I suspect we soon got over the shock, and Denise quickly became part of our family group. And a better included family I swear never existed. We did everything together. No problem was too large, no difficulty insurmountable. I cannot recall that my being a disabled person ever restricted our activities.

For any distance walking and away days, I used a manual wheelchair, as walking on my artificial legs was getting harder and harder. I always had plenty of help for negotiating steps and stairs from my family and friends. The local cinema allowed me to sit parked in my chair at the back of the stalls if there were no end of the aisle seats available. And my parents saw no reason why I should not accompany them to restaurants and other social events.

To put this into perspective, you must remember that in this era, the 1960s, it was far more likely that disabled people would be cloistered away in isolation, out of sight and often out of mind. I was not. And the world could like it or lump it as far as my family were concerned. I was the only obviously disabled person at most of these events and I fancy I relished my 'star' status.

I soon got used to the stares; people will stare, you know, and it was my sisters who used to get uptight about it. But it was not always that easy for me. Anyone who has had the unfortunate experience of having a pimple on their nose can understand how people have their gaze drawn inexorably toward it. And for me, I was a permanent pimple to them. Not always a very comfortable feeling, even though you had to make the best of it.

I think that Thalidomide-impaired people did a lot to help the Disabled People's Movement in that respect, because suddenly we were there, we were mixing with other people and we were not going to go away.

When people would stare at me, my sisters would glare back at them, and if the perpetrators continued to offend, Debbie or Denise would ask them, with hands on hips and cocky attitude, if they would like to take a photograph! They were just being protective and felt equally as uncomfortable as I did when being stared at. For my part I just got used to being stared at, which does not mean to say that I enjoyed it. My reaction would be very different from the girls'. When people stared at me, I would look them straight in the face and smile. This provoked one of two reactions; either they would look away embarrassed or they would smile back.

However, deep in my sub-conscience I must have felt incredibly uncomfortable at being stared at. I kept having a recurring nightmare of thousands of pairs of eyes, no faces, just eyes with voices. You know those kind of dreams that even when you wake up, and with your eyes wide open, you are still in that dream.

One night though, when I think I was about fifteen years old, I was having one of these nightmares, and suddenly a wave of bravado came over me. I told the eyes to go away, that I was no longer afraid of them, and unless they had a useful purpose, they were not to come back again. From that day to this, I have not had this nightmare!

The psychologist in me explains this in terms of my coming to accept who I am, what I look like and not worrying about other people's reactions to the way I look!

It was not an easy ride, and yes, I too experienced discrimination and physical abuse. The two most horrible I can recall happened at school. I absolutely hate cabbage. I cannot stand the smell or taste, and coming from an Irish family background that is a bit of an irony. Anyway, it regularly turned up as one of the dishes at school dinners, and I always declined. However, one day a member of staff decided that I must have some. I explained that I would not be able to eat it, that it would make me ill. But the more I protested the more she insisted, to the extent that she force fed me with the cabbage. Consequently, when I did get sick, she force fed me with that as well.

On another occasion, although I was a day girl rather than a border at school, when we were performing the school plays at Christmas time, particularly for our families in the evening, we were expected to have a rest in the afternoon. One of the so-called 'carers' got us out of bed, lined up about six of us, and brushed our hair with a hairbrush that belonged to a girl who had lice. The others just seemed to accept it, but I strongly protested. Perhaps

I should have kept my mouth shut – literally. Because she then went on to clean our teeth. Yes, you guessed it, with the same toothbrush.

When I was about eleven, my youngest sister Denise, who could barely see over the back of my wheelchair, took me to a corner shop, near my Grandmother's. The aisle was too narrow for my chair, so she parked me out of the way while she went to the back of the shop to pick out some birthday cards. Before she could come back, the shopkeeper came round and started pushing me out the door. There was a huge step and he had no intention of tipping the chair back properly. Denise literally sprinted over, physically lifted the man, pulled him out of the way and grabbed the back of my chair and my hair, which was the only thing that stopped me falling flat on my face on the pavement.

I could not understand why he did it. What was his problem? I wasn't shoplifting or breaking anything. I was not in the way, or blocking the door or the aisle, or the counter. I was just sitting there, minding my own business. In many respects it was physical abuse, throwing me out like that, because I came so close to hitting the pavement! I was shocked at the time, but it' is only as an adult that I realise the full implications of it all. I could have been very seriously hurt, but I don't think he even gave it any thought. It was just, 'I don't like you. I don't like the way you look, and I don't want you in here upsetting my customers. Therefore I am going to throw you out.' My family boycotted that shop afterwards. We always used to walk past it to another corner shop and sometimes gave two fingers and raspberries along the way! The people at the other shop were fine.

Later, when I was about twelve or thirteen, I was shopping one day with my Mum and my two sisters. Mum had seen a new boutique open at the top end of Albany Road, a shopping area not far from home, so we all went in and were looking round when all of a sudden the woman came from behind the counter and said, "Get out, get out, get out!"

When we asked why, she said, "Can't you read? Haven't you seen the sign on the door? No prams allowed."

I said, "This is not a pram. This is my wheelchair. This is how I get around."

The woman said, "Well I don't care. You are ruining my new carpet!"

We were all so shocked we left the shop. And as we walked up the road, I could hear my Mum crying behind me. I was angry and upset as well, but I was even madder because Mum was upset. We all wanted to go back and sort the woman out, but Nana and Papa Moriarty lived not far away, so we went there instead to have a cup of tea and calm down.

I felt OK about being disabled, but obviously it was not always OK for other people. Incidents like these do stick in your mind because they are unpleasant. There were lots of nice experiences, but I think you remember the horrible ones more. I was never wrapped up in cotton wool by my family. But because I did so much with them and because I was so loved, when other people – total strangers or people working in supposed caring roles – did those things to me, it felt like a real imposition. At the same time, I think things like that eventually make you tougher. Now as an adult, there is no way I would let anybody treat me like that. But as a child you do not always question, especially when it is an adult behaving like that towards you.

As a family we made trips on the ferry to Ireland, which always entailed visiting family and friends. Maisie, Michael and our cousins Rosemary, Michelle and Raymond lived in the countryside just outside Killmallock, County Limerick. I have many happy memories of those holidays, including being dragged up innumerable flights of stairs into smoky dance halls where we would all enjoy listening to a live band and I would watch people in sophisticated acts involving Irish dancing or the jive.

I enjoyed it, even though such dancing would never be for me.

The dancing may have been physical enough, but it was as nothing compared with my struggling to get around on my artificial limbs. It was exhausting work and, determinedly independent as I was, a far from satisfactory business. Even going a modest distance would be both a sweaty and exhausting affair, leaving me drained for the rest of the day, so it was with some glee that, on one of my trips to the Nuffield Orthopaedic Hospital, I spotted a mechanical marvel: an electrically powered wheelchair! It was standing, clearly abandoned, in a corridor and, working on the age–old principle, "Them as don't ask, don't get," I asked if I could have it.

Probably shocked at such a request from a nine-year-old, the staff assented. It had been used by an old lady up until the time that she had carelessly driven it into a pond. And it was now, presumably dried out, it was up for grabs. With that lack of thought typical of most young girls of my age, I quite forgot to ask if the old lady had survived the immersion. The chair clearly had. The batteries were charged, and, after taking a test drive up and down the corridor, it was formally handed over into my keeping. My parents gave me a wide berth in it until I had the hang of the thing. A truly liberating moment!

By now we had moved to a new and bigger house in Sturminster Road in Cardiff. There were fewer friends for me there, but a few doors down, Karen Rideout became another sister to me and spent more time in our house than in her own. Years later she became a nurse and told me that she put it down to spending so much time with me then.

After nine exhausting years, Mum and Dad for once went off on a holiday on their own, the first since their honeymoon. They must have needed it. Auntie Nancy and Uncle Tony, who as always came up trumps in terms of supporting the family, looked after Denise who was a little toddler by now. Debbie and I went to stay with our so-called Auntie Mattie at her bungalow in Cowbridge. She was only an auntie in name, just a friend of the family. She ran the Jane Hodge Holiday Home where I had stayed on a few occasions. This was in the little hamlet of Trerhyngyll, in the heart of the Vale of Glamorgan. It was an area of rolling farmland leading down to what would later become the Glamorgan Heritage Coast, a coastline with a mixture of dramatic beaches and rocky shores. The steep, plunging cliffs, tiny secluded coves and breathtaking views made the area an unforgettable sight for me.

We went along to a fund-raising night for the home, and they sat me on a table so that I could conduct the Treochy Male Voice Choir. Whether my conducting improved their performance at all I rather doubt, but they succeeded in spite of me, and the night was pronounced a success.

While we were staying with Auntie Mattie, Neil Armstrong landed on the moon. Watching the event by way of the blurry television images, it occurred to me that his efforts of walking on the moon were uncannily similar to mine on Earth.

Back to school and a year or so later, more as a gesture than with any hope of success, we were set a series of tests, something akin to the dreaded eleven plus examination in the early 1970s. No doubt to the astonishment of the staff, six of us passed and were thus qualified to move (at the appropriate time) up into the school next door, St Cyrus Comprehensive. Unfortunately, the school proved to be not comprehensive enough since there was no access for wheelchairs. Bev and I were stuck in our old school, the first of many such setbacks for us, even with our electrically driven wheelchairs.

Summer holidays provided some consolation, and apart from visiting relatives in Ireland, we occasionally got adventurous. I recall one such trip that Debbie and I went on, in the shape of a sort of outward bound course, with camping, craftwork and 'walks' on Dartmoor, organised I believe by the Lady Hoare Trust. The next year the whole family went to Pevendsey in Hampshire where the family of another

Thalidomide boy, Tom Yendell, ran a guest house that was set up to cater for disabled people. It was the first of many visits to places where we and other 'Thalidomide families,' could socialise with a wider range of our fellows and gain encouragement from their efforts. We were no longer the odd ones out.

## My Best Friend

My best friend comes everywhere with me.
My best friend is as faithful as could be,
My best friend does not answer back —
I bet you haven't got a best friend like that!

My best friend is not ugly — in fact,
My best friend is handsome and strong.
My best friend can do nothing wrong.
You see — my best friend is my wheelchair!

By

Rosaleen Moriarty-Simmonds

1980

# 10.

# Learning...to Be Me

*Rosie and Beverley – the 'terrible twins' – on a school trip.*

It took from February 1963 until August 1973 to complete the Thalidomide litigation in this country. It was hard enough for our parents to bring us up under unusual circumstances, added to which they had to battle with the drug company, Distillers Company (Biochemicals) Ltd.

It must have been something akin to that scene in the Bible of 'David versus Goliath.'

Distillers used every dirty trick in the book to undermine, discredit, pressurise and blackmail our parents and anyone who attempted to support them. Distillers had the financial backing and the most expensive and aggressive legal and public relations teams. Often it seemed to the parents that Distillers also had the Government, the legal system, the press and above all — 'time' on their side.

Our parents had the everyday hardship of bringing up disabled children in a world that was not designed for disabled people. Many struggled to scrape together enough money so that they could allege negligence and claim damages against the company.

An offer was made to the sixty-two families who had issued writs, but only in return for their withdrawing claims of negligence against the company. The offer only provided for 40 per cent of the legal valuation of our injuries. Hardly an over-generous offer, but one which the cash strapped families had little option but to accept. As a public relations ploy, the company said that they would make future provision to compensate all those that had been affected by the drug. However, most of their proposal proved to be unsatisfactory, and it was not until 1973 that agreement was reached. A total of 440 children withdrew their negligence claims in return for compensation.

The *London Times* hailed it as something of a victory, saying that the settlement had "Avoided the expense of a long and expensive trial". The paper did, however, also point out that the award was some 40 per cent of what we claimants might have received had we been successful in court.

The *Daily Mirror* reported it as being "An excellent outcome," and went on to say, "Distillers Company has clearly done its best to be understanding, humane and generous." They failed to point out that had not an anguished parent taken some action, the company's understanding, humanity and generosity would have been unlikely to surface.

As it was, the directors and shareholders of Distillers must have breathed a sigh of relief. The affair would merely show up as a tick mark in the annual accounts, a mere fleabite in the profit margin, and they were now free from any allegations of negligence.

The settlement was praised as being, "Appreciated by every firm and every medical researcher seeking to alleviate human suffering by research on new drugs," ignoring the fact that the tragedy had been the result of a lack of or shoddy research and that the principal object had been the generation of profits.

As with the initial sixty-two families, compensation was offered to the remainder at a value of 40 per cent of assessed damages. Distillers further agreed to pay money into a trust fund which was to augment the individual settlements. It was for this purpose that the Thalidomide Trust was created.

Our battle-weary parents must have felt isolated and incongruent in their opinions of Distillers, the Law, the Media, the Government and the public. But not everyone sat on their laurels and just expected the parents to get on with it. I am certainly aware of one brave young group of university students here in Wales who started a 'poster campaign' in support of our parents. At the dead of night, they would seek out any of the Distillers advertising posters for some of their other products, such as Johnny Walker whisky and Gordon's gin, and paste defamatory slogans across them.

In addition, in the December 1972 edition of *Phoenix*, the University College Cardiff magazine, a hard-hitting fourteen-page, article by 'Openeye' was printed: 'Thalidomide in Wales'. I remember the writer coming to interview Mum, Dad and me.

Between 1961 and 1974, there had been no occasion where a Thalidomide child was not before the court, and throughout this time the drug company used *sub judice* laws to preclude any serious discussion on the Thalidomide cases because Distillers thought it would prejudice their case if details were printed in the press or talked about on television. Anyone found doing so could have been fined or imprisoned. But the students were prepared to take the risk.

Whilst all this was going on, my parents were also concerned about my education.

"She must have an education, Mena," said my father, discussing my future with my mother. "She's bright – look at the IQ results. And that school's not doing it for her."

Although I am sure he was pleased with the dramatic abilities that I had shown at Erw'r Delyn, he was a great believer in book learning.

It was decided to use some of my entitlement from the Thalidomide Trust to fund a private tutor for reading, writing and maths.

And so, twice a week, I was subjected to the agony of learning. Although it would have been nothing out of the ordinary for an ordinary student; unfortunately, I was not ordinary. For a start, even had I any inclination for reading, the physical struggle of dealing with a book was almost insurmountable. I had no means to hold it (nowadays I use a series of book stands designed for cookery books), and page turning was completely beyond me. The classics would have to wait I felt. But eventually I decided that there was nothing for it; I had to use my tongue to turn the pages!

Writing was almost as bad. Having long since ditched my gas-powered arms, with which I could not write at all. Balancing the pen between my two fingers whilst leaning it against my chin to steady it, meant that my eyes were so close to the paper that I went cockeyed in the effort. And what an effort it was just to scratch a few lines!

As with most things in life, it is practise that you need, and, never having had much of it in the academic line, I found the going extremely tough. Maths was a mystery to me (they still are) and a spelling test just caused my brain to freeze over.

After tea, Dad would sometimes conduct an impromptu quiz on our knowledge of the times tables. Firing questions, he expected us to be able to respond instantly. Easy enough for Debbie, who could usually get the answer off pat. But for me, my brain would turn to jelly and beads of sweat would appear on my forehead in fear. And I dare not look Dad in the eye. It was, of course, only my lack of familiarity with being questioned on things I was not confident about which caused my thought processes to freeze. I'm sure Dad understood. However, he would feign his displeasure.

"Rosie, it should be easy for you. Look at me. I have to think of the answer in Gaelic and then translate it into English. You have only to make the one step," he would say.

But it was not much of a consolation, and I continued to dread the inquisitions.

On a more positive note, my social life was on the up and up. Although I had my sisters, many cousins and primarily Debbie's school friends to have fun with, joining St Joseph's Youth Club was a good move. Particularly so because we came into contact with boys. This was fairly new territory for me, mixing with boys who were neither related nor disabled. It also brought mixed blessings, because for the first time ever I questioned what I looked like.

I can't recall as a child ever thinking that I looked or was different from other people because it never was a big issue. However, things changed when I moved from childhood into my early teens, you know that stage when you first start becoming aware of what you look like, your image and you start to become interested in the opposite sex. I would look in the mirror and see a round chubby girl with two fingers coming from each shoulder, short little legs, long black hair, blue eyes and a friendly face - but a face that was covered in acne and on top of that eczema. Believe it or not, I was more anxious about the acne and the eczema than I was about the missing limbs!

Debbie and I made some great friends at St Joseph's Youth Club: the Maunders, Patersons, Lewis's, Colemans and Regans. We would hang out at each other's houses, take day trips to the beach and go under-age drinking together. As a teenager you do go through phases of fancying your mates, which is dodgy because it can backfire if the relationship goes pear shaped. I soon realised that none of the guys fancied me but were more than happy to be my friend. And that was mostly cool. I could understand their position. I did look different from any other teenager. Having said that, I would like to say thanks to Kevin and Mark, who at some party or other did not leave me out of the equation when it came to communal kisses!

From as early an age as my parents thought I could understand, they explained to me what had caused my impairments. They always answered any questions I had as truthfully as they could. Actually being different, as far as I'm concerned, is not a negative thing but a positive thing. It's what makes me unique.

The new decade of the 1970s had ushered in something of a change in the official attitude toward disabled people in Society. Rather than being shoved away out of sight, like unwanted clothes in a closet, there was a move afoot to see if there could be a use for us in everyday life. And the first priority had to be that of education.

Perhaps my father had been prescient in this, for shortly after I started the agonies of learning, a new and enlightened headmaster was appointed to my school in 1974.

George Crabbe arrived at Erw'r Delyn School with a whole new outlook on the education of his charges. At a meeting with him, Dad, Mum and Bev's parents made it known to him that, because of our wheelchair-using existence, we were being deprived of opportunities that were really our due. The level of education we were receiving was falling far behind our abilities through no fault of our own.

Mr Crabbe listened carefully, agreeing wholeheartedly with their point of view and promised to look into it. Unlike most of those in his position who promise so glibly, he actually delivered.

Pulling strings, he arranged for us to have a trial run (so to speak) at the Florence Treloar School in Hampshire in January of the next year.

So my fourteenth birthday in December 1974 was something of a celebration with friends and relatives clustering around at our home.

It was to be the start of a new era in my life.

# 11.

# Welcome to Holybourne: Treloar Awaits

*A view of the former Florence Treloar School for Girls, now the Treloar College at Alton, Hampshire.*

I n 1907 the Lord Mayor of the City of London, Sir
William Purdie Treloar, decided to do something
to help London's 'crippled children'. His aim was
to build a hospital and teaching facility outside the
city for children with non-pulmonary tuberculosis,
which was all too common among the poor in the
early 1900s. He set up his 'Cripples Fund' as his
mayoral appeal and recorded in his diary that on 13
June 1907 Her Majesty Queen Alexandra 'came to
Mansion House to open the Queen's Fete in aid of my
Cripples Fund.' Later the facilities were expanded to
include all disabled children.

I am very grateful to him, for in January 1975 Bev
and I went to Holybourne, near Alton in Hampshire,
to test the delights of the school there. It was a
fee-paying grammar-level boarding school with
separate colleges for boys and girls. But because our
educational requirements could not be met within the
county, the fees for sending us to Treloar's were paid
for by our local education authority.

Bev and I spent one week there, our first experience
of the rigours and ardours of a boarding school, and
one that left us shell-shocked. It was all so alien to
our life so far, and our horror was compounded when
it was decreed that, having been accepted into the
portals of that establishment following our trial week,
we would be despatched there forthwith to further
our education.

Protesting loudly, we were bundled off and found
that, for the first time, we were going to be separated.
Bev was some months older than I and remained with
her age group whilst I was demoted down a year. Each
group had its own common rooms and dormitories,

and we were not allowed to access the others. So, sadly, the 'terrible twins' came to be separated. A price to be paid for our education I suppose, but we had considered ourselves inseparable until then. Like a good many kids who get shovelled off to boarding school, we were hardly appreciative of our new regime: bells ringing for everything, posh accents, interminable rules and regulations with timetables for everything; even sleeping and eating were done to order. To us new girls, it was Dante's Inferno brought into our world.

But the homesickness wore off, as it does, and slowly we came to appreciate that being a student at Treloar's was quite an honour and a privilege.

Suddenly maths seemed less daunting, and reading no longer seemed impossible but even desirable.

My academic skills started to rise in the new situation. Perhaps it was the fact that I was now in a more competitive environment where I could measure my abilities against those who were very much my peers, and I was determined not to be left behind.

Now the efforts that my parents had made to allow me to live as normal a life as was possible paid off, for the social opportunities that now presented themselves to me were beyond my wildest dreams. I had probably had more exposure to the wide world than most of my fellows, and the field trips and educational visits laid on by the school were meat and drink to me.

Visits to the Albert Hall were a regular feature, and I was among those who were chosen to join the choir of one hundred children to sing there for the production of *Joseph and his Amazing Technicolour*

*Dreamcoat*. Modestly, I refrained from mentioning that I had conducted the Treochy Male Voice Choir on a previous occasion and that merely being a member of the choir was thus something of a demotion.

The school offered so much that I soon forgot my separation from Bev and my distress at being away from home. This was ameliorated by being quite close to the home of my Uncle Peter and Auntie Avis Lacey. Actually, technically he was a great-uncle, my maternal grandmother's youngest brother, but I had spent two wonderful weeks during the previous summer holidays with them before going to Florence Treloar. On one of many day trips during that fortnight we went to the Isle of Wight on the hovercraft service, all of us, eleven kids (that is me, my sister Debbie and cousin Ann and the eight Lacey children) and two adults, squeezed into a Volkswagen van. During that day I had noticed that Uncle Peter got through a whole bottle of cough mixture. Unbeknown to me, he had lung cancer. Sadly, he died shortly after I arrived at the school; meanwhile, I had been able to visit him every weekend, trying to make his remaining time a little more comfortable. I would tempt him to take the odd spoonful of soup, even though he didn't really want it. Even when he could hardly talk and despite the excruciating pain he was in, his zest for life and fun was still there, and his bright blue eyes sparkled whenever he saw me.

Afterwards, almost every weekend, Auntie Avis would collect me from school and take me home to their house. I became their ninth child, with my own bed there for me whenever I wanted it.

And, of course, holidays were spent with my family. For two years running we went to a Pontins Holiday Camp, which provided much of the sort of amenities that I needed.

Thinking back to being a teenager, I was fourteen, and I was madly in love with a boy who went to school with my sister. Of course, I was at Treloar and Debbie was at mainstream school. She had sack loads of Valentine cards, and I wondered where were mine. I do remember getting a Valentine card, and I was told it was from the boy I was in love with. I still don't know to this day whether it really was from him or whether it was from Debbie being kind!

I was starting to think that boys were not that bad, but then I realised that they just wanted to be friends. They didn't want to snog me, in the way that they were snogging my sister and cousins and other friends of the same age. That was when I realised that I did look different. And although making friends was not an issue, I suddenly thought, 'Am I ever going to get a boyfriend? Is anybody ever going to look at me and love me for who I am? Can they see beyond the missing arms and legs and get to know the real me, Rosie?'

That is an image thing right across the board for disabled people because we live in a world where what you look like is the most important thing. The body beautiful image, slim, blonde, blue eyes - all these things are so important, and all of a sudden you think 'Well, I don't fit into any of those boxes.'

When I was fifteen, the local paper, the *Western Mail*, ran a story on me, along with a picture of me in my wheelchair hanging out with my cousin Jimmy. The article began:

"Being a bridesmaid at a white wedding is one of the romantic dreams of most girls," it said. "And Rose Moriarty plans to look as pretty as a picture for a family wedding next spring. 'I may even paint my wheelchair white and stick confetti all over it,' she jokes."

But it was not as a bridesmaid that I dreamed of being at a wedding. It was as a bride, and sometimes that dream seemed to be just that – an impossible dream.

Not that I dwelt on it. But have you ever felt that you are in a crowded room and you know everybody there and you are all good friends yet you still feel lonely? That was when I wrote a poem called 'Transient Despair!' Now I laugh when I read it because it is so not me. But on the day I wrote it, I must have been really fed up because it is so sad. That was the first time I ever put any feelings on paper. Don't get me wrong; I haven't written hundreds of poems. I might write two poems in one day and then five years later write another one! But being able to put your feelings on paper helps. In that respect it was a good cathartic experience. 'Get it out of your system, girl, and move on, for God's sake, or otherwise you'll be stuck here forever!'

Just before going off to boarding school, I liberated myself from using artificial legs in favour of permanently using my very practical electric-powered wheelchair or being pushed around by others in my manual wheelchair. I did, however, continue to use cosmetic legs, the frequency of which declined as I got older, to use only on special occasions. The last time was my wedding day!

I think I had more fun with the cosmetic artificial limbs after the age of fourteen than I had ever done so before. If I wore jeans, I did not need to use the Velcro strap to keep the legs on. So, if I went out anywhere and I needed to whip them off quickly (to go to the toilet or get into a car), whoever was with me would just have to grab the ankle and pull them down the trouser leg!

On one occasion when I was going to a Thalidomide Society conference with Denise, we travelled by train. Ironically, the conference was about artificial limbs. The train journey itself was an experience, travelling in the guard's van. Anyway, we were late for our connection, and Denise was running along the platform pushing me when at some stage we must have gone over a drawing pin, which caused a puncture. She spent the rest of our time in the train (in another guard's van) stopping my chair from spinning around. We finally arrived at Runcorn and had to get a taxi to the hotel. The taxi driver decided that he would be able to get me in my wheelchair into his taxi, but after numerous attempts, he failed. By which time Denise was losing the will to live. In her impatience she just whipped my legs off and threw them into the taxi. She then picked me up and threw me into the taxi, followed by the wheelchair. At that point we looked around only to see that the taxi driver had passed out and was flat on the floor!

On another occasion, whilst spending some time with my Lacey cousins in Aldershot, my cousin Sheila thought it would be a good idea for me to borrow her skirt instead of wearing jeans all the time. (Sheila and Mary were closest to me in age, and the ones who helped me with all of my personal requirements, dressing, toileting and so forth whenever I stayed there.) We were going to a disco that night, so we all got dolled up. My cousin Mary was pushing me at high speed because, as usual, we were running late. The wind caught the skirt and lifted it up over my head. Cars started screeching and honking their horns, and I was screaming at Mary to slow down and pull my skirt down. It seemed like an eternity before Sheila noticed what had happened and finally gave me back my modesty!

Another time whilst out shopping with Mary, we were coming out the back of Woolworths in Aldershot. She tilted the wheelchair back to get me down the two steps. Again, I was wearing a skirt but with no strap, and one of the legs just went flying off, bounced down the steps and landed on the pavement. You know those moments when you don't know whether to laugh or cry? Well, I thought I would die with embarrassment. I wanted the ground to open up and swallow me, particularly as a group of squaddies were coming towards us. I was left gobsmacked when one of the squaddies picked up my leg, placed it across the arms of my wheelchair and said, "I think this is yours, love." And off they went into the wilderness. By this time Mary was sat on the pavement whooping with laughter.

Then there was a trip to Ireland to my cousin Rosemary's wedding. I had worn the legs all day and wanted a bit of freedom. Although my Mum preferred me to wear the legs, it was a hot night, and she agreed that I could take them off. Deborah and Denise were assigned the task of sneaking them out to discreetly put them in our minibus. About half an hour later, my uncle Michael came in laughing hysterically. What the girls had actually done was to place the legs in the back window of our minibus in such a way that it looked as if some youngsters were having hanky-panky in the back of the minibus! The scene had caused quite a stir, and my uncle had been outside watching people arriving for the evening wedding party bewildered, amused and, of course, somewhat shocked by the scene before them. Apparently, some guests had almost crashed their cars in the car park whilst watching the supposed antics in the minibus rather than keeping their eyes on the road.

These are fun memories of my mid-teens. And all in all, life was pretty good for Rosie Moriarty – or I would make it so.

# Transient Despair

Anaesthetised — is the word I'm looking for.
Nil, nonplus, negative, locked up behind a big black door.
Hidden behind a mask, a false smiling mask,
"Good old Rosie," I hear them say,
"Always happy," "Always smiling,"
God if only they knew.
Don't misinterpret or misjudge me, I'm not drowning in self-pity or cracking up.
No! I don't need a pity — I deplore it.
And I don't need a psychologist — I can cajole myself without one of them.
All I advocate is your understanding, intellect, insight, agreement, stipulation and tolerance.
Do you hear what I am saying?
I'm confused, probably expecting too much out of life, and this crazy mixed up world.
I'm an adult — I think.
Please tell me who I am and what I want.
I need love — not parental love, or sexual love.
I feel nothing today — no love, no hate — no happiness, no sadness.
I need a key to my big black door.
I'm anaesthetised — yes, that's the word I'm looking for.


By
Rosaleen Moriarty-Simmonds
1980

# 12.

# Growing Up

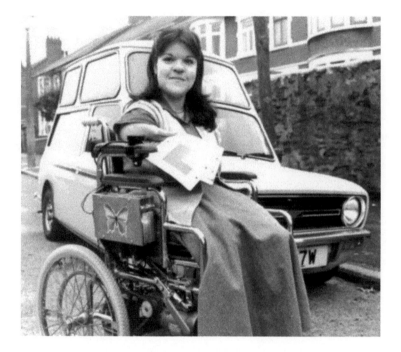

*November 1982, no longer an L's Angel!*

I n my three and one-half years at Florence Treloar School, I had caught up so well academically that I was able to boast of O-levels, CSEs and RSAs.

It had been hard work, I must admit, but now it was time for me to move on.

During the period from 1974 to 1979, many changes had been made in our family home. It was the wise use of my interest in the Thalidomide Trust that resulted in two major alterations. A kitchen/ dining room extension provided more room for our grown-up family and my need for space to manoeuvre around. Later the double garage at the side of our house was demolished to make way for a two-storey extension. This addition gave me a living room of my own and above provided Dad with much needed office space. The upstairs was arranged so that live-in support could be made available for me at a future date. My parents had the foresight to consider my care needs at a very early stage, but that (rightly or wrongly) presupposed that I would stay with them as I progressed in age.

Now having got the studying bug, I enrolled in a one-year business studies course at Hereward College, Coventry, where I hoped to obtain a BEC general certificate.

Hereward was fully equipped to handle students like me as residents. But the College also gave us opportunities to mix with non-disabled students and residents from the local area. This struck me as being a very sensible approach and made the social side of life there considerably more interesting.

The first person I got talking to was Val Stephenson, and we soon became lifetime friends.

My roommate was Janette Mottley, who became another lifelong friend. And between us we had not a pair of arms or legs!

To celebrate my eighteenth birthday, we had a family celebration back home in Cardiff, which we had to hold in the local St Joseph's Church Hall in order to fit everybody in. I had dragged some college friends home with me, and all of my St Joseph's friends and extended family were there.

Every weekend at college was pub night at the Woody's, which provided a welcome relief from some pretty hard studying. I received the ultimate accolade for any female student – I won the kissing competition at the college Christmas party. I had to kiss quite a few frogs along the way though before I found my prince!! It was such fun being young, free, single, having a good snog with loads of blokes and coming out the winner. That was a wonderful experience for me.

After earning my BEC general certificate in business studies, I enrolled for a second year at Hereward College to do some more O-levels. That year I seemed to have missed out in the kissing competition, however. My interest in politics was enhanced when I was voted vice president of the student union, and a very interesting weekend was spent in Blackpool at the National Union of Students conference.

Now it was time to go back home and it was with mixed and confusing feelings. Obviously, I loved being at home with my family, but I also relished the independence and freedom that I had enjoyed whilst living away at school and college.

My circle of friends had changed dramatically. When you move away from home, things do not stand still in your city. Everybody else moves on as well. The good friends that I had made at St Joseph's Youth Club were now more akin to acquaintances. During term time my friends were my fellow students. During holiday time my friends were my sister Debbie's friends. Throughout my lifetime I have had friends whose impairments were also caused by the drug Thalidomide. Some I got to know when we were babies and children in hospital; others, at school and college; others, through the Thalidomide Society AGM and Conference weekends; and still others, through organised holidays.

In the mid-1970s the Thalidomide Trust Fund purchased Haighmoor House, a small hotel on the Island if Jersey, and adapted it for disabled residents. Here, many Thalidomide-impaired people and their families had holidays. More important, we met others with the same impairments as ours, and we learnt a lot from each other about how to cope with our conditions. Many friendships and, indeed, some relationships were formed on these holidays. I have met and become friends with a great number of Thalidomide-impaired people.

On one such holiday, we met the Freeman family: Ted, Beattie and their son Eddie. The uncanny thing about Eddie is that his impairments are almost identical to mine. Our families enjoyed each other's company so much so that we would synchronise diaries to make sure that we were at Haighmoor at the same time.

We are still great friends. Eddie is a cartoonist and has drawn many of the cartoons that I use when delivering Disability Equality Training workshops and lectures. Eddie calls me his Little Sis and I call him my Big Bro.

In the summer of 1980, the Thalidomide Trust organised the first of many holidays abroad for those adventurous Thalidomide-impaired people who wished to travel. The cost would be taken from the personal allocations of each of the Thalidomide-impaired people travelling and would pay not only for our flights and accommodation but also for the young and fit men and women that accompanied us to assist us.

So, whilst the rest of my family went to Tralee in Ireland for the Rose of Tralee Festival, at which my sister Debbie represented South Wales, I went off to Gran Canaria. And a wonderful time was had by one and all. Between 1980 and 1987, I travelled to Tenerife and Yugoslavia, toured Europe and visited America twice.

World travel was therefore definitely on the agenda. Pontins was bypassed in favour of the rather more exotic delights of Disney World in Florida. Hitting the high spots in New York, Miami and Orlando was an experience both for me and for the citizens of America, I imagine.

The Disney World people must have had visions of personal injury lawsuits dancing in their heads when they saw me, along with a fellow traveller, Iain McGhie, being strapped into our seats for a trip on Space Mountain. And if there was one advantage we had over the rest of the visitors, it was that we didn't have to stand in line and queue for hours.

Interspersed between all this travelling one still had to study, of course. So, in September 1980 I enrolled in the local College, on Colchester Avenue, now part of the University of Wales Institute, Cardiff, to study for a two-year BEC national diploma, once again in business studies.

On my first morning there, I made a grand entrance in my electric chair, but unfortunately being momentarily distracted, I cannoned into the first desk in spectacular fashion. Visions of the little old lady driving it into the pond flashed through my mind. It is fair to say that I made a significant impression on my fellow students that morning.

Notably, when I would appear on the scene in my racing machine, the crowds parted, rather in the manner of the Red Sea on an earlier Biblical occasion, to allow me access and, I suspect, to safeguard their toes.

This minor triumph apart, I was now finding that I was a match for my peers when it came to the cerebral side of affairs. Accepting that it was the only way to compete, I went at it with a will and an enthusiasm that I doubted they could match.

At long last I realised that, academically, I was now an equal with my non-disabled peers. And as for making friends, well, that came easy. Once people get over the shock or at least surprise at the way I look and get to know me as a person, they accept Rosie for who she is. Friends quite often tell me that the more they get to know me, they forget the fact that I don't have any arms or legs!

And that was certainly also the way with my college mates. Geraldine Doyle moved across to make way for me to sit next to her on that first morning, and we remained firm friends whilst at college. Jonathan was a sweet, shy guy. When he discovered that he lived not far from me, he would often pop in for a chat or we'd listen to music. Anthony Abraham, the joker in the class, took great joy in pulling my ponytail or deactivating my electric wheelchair! Our paths crossed again in recent years when our children attended the same school. I knew it was him by the tug on my hair!

At home, with my accommodation now in place (and very comfortable and convenient it was, too), there was still the expectation that this is where I would remain, sheltered and protected from the vicissitudes of a cruel world. I hated to disillusion my family, but Rosie Moriarty had tasted life and was determined to make her own way, painful or not. And it was a good five years since I had had my first cigarette and my first kiss – not at the same time though. I was an emancipated young lady, just lacking a few of the more usual accoutrements. But why should that stop me?

I gave serious thought as to how I should make my way in the world. Having diplomas and certificates was all well and good, but I felt that I would need more to impress any prospective employer. And after a few years of business studies, I was not only bored with the subject (who wouldn't be?) but also felt it was not the be all and end all of my life, just a basis that I would be able to build upon in the future, once, of course, I had decided what that might be. Then, one lecturer seeing that I was a 'people watcher,' suggested that I applied for a place at university to read psychology.

Being near to home was a comforting thought, both on the practical and the financial front. So I applied to both Cardiff University and the University of Wales – at that time more correctly known as the University of Wales Science and Technology, or UWIST.

Waiting for the results of my application, I turned my thoughts to yet another way of asserting my independence. I would learn to drive. And this time not an electric chair, but a real motorcar.

The prospect of being able to drive my own car as my contemporaries did seemed like only a pipedream. Firstly, it required a genius to invent a car that someone without arms or legs could drive. Secondly, I would have to convince Mum and Dad that it was a good idea also. My lucky break came when we were at our annual Thalidomide Society AGM and Conference weekend. Part of the conference was about adapted cars for disabled people. And they even had a converted mini on display which had been adapted for someone with my degree of impairment.

Mum and Dad were convinced. Two years later, in September 1982, after many enquiries, a number of tests and fittings, lots of delays and teething problems, Dad, Bob (my driving instructor) and I went to collect 'Mavis' and have my first driving lesson in a hotel car park. The British School of Motoring undertook to give me lessons, and I imagine that the instructors drew straws or were offered danger money for the job. Probably since no one volunteered, it was one of the senior instructors who gave me my first lesson.

'Mavis' was my pet name for my cream-coloured mini clubman with its extended roof, which made it look like the 'PopeMobile'. 'Mavis' was so-called because the car registration number was MAV 7W. The controls were incredible. The steering was done via a computerised joystick. The brakes and accelerator I controlled with my left foot in an extended stirrup (push down for brakes and raise up for accelerator). The gears were automatic. On the extended hand brake was a control box with buttons for the lights, indicator, horn and other devices. The back doors were replaced by a lift which took me and my electric chair from ground level up, and I bolted my electric chair in behind the front seats. On the back of the passenger seat was a platform, on to which I would waddle before hurling myself into the driver's seat. At my request, it was designed to give me complete independence.

Six weeks and twenty-four lessons later, I passed my driving test first time. When Bob and I pulled up outside the house, Mum was already on the doorstep waiting for us. We had decided, as a tease, to pretend I had failed. I tried to keep a straight face, but I was so excited I could have burst. Mum was hugging and kissing me. In fact, everyone was hugging and kissing; even our dog Kerry was going mad. In her usual fashion, Mum sent the telephone bill soaring by ringing everyone in the phone book to tell them. There were, I am sure, a good many grey hairs amongst the instruction team by then, and the stories of the case will be passed down from generation to generation. "I was Rosie Moriarty's instructor" is a badge of courage and an inspiration for all newcomers to their profession.

I cannot put into words how I felt later that day, when for the first time ever I went out completely 'on my own'. It was like taking the first step on the moon, like discovering a new land and like being liberated all rolled into one feeling. Where previously even getting to college and then university was down to Mum, 'Mavis' opened up a whole new world for me. I no longer had to depend on family and friends to get me from A to B.

The local paper ran a story on me, complete with a picture of me grinning like a Cheshire cat in front of 'Mavis'.

Many fun times were had in that car, outings with friends (the most people in the car at one time was five), courting down lovers lane in Roath Park, shopping with Mum, getting myself to university and work.

I am prepared to admit that I have absolutely no sense of direction, and, if driving in an unfamiliar area, passengers have had to give me directions. If Debbie or Denise travel with me, they even tell me which lane to go in or inform me that the lights are red. (I can't imagine why.) On one such occasion, Denise was in the passenger seat and our cousin Teresa was travelling in the back – sitting in my wheelchair. Denise, giving directions, said, "Take the second turning off the roundabout. It's a sharp bend and goes straight up hill." By way of explanation, to get 'Mavis' up any hill required putting your foot down. I duly obliged, and to everyone's astonishment took the corner on two wheels. The G-force took us all to the right, so not only did the car go on two wheels but so did the wheelchair in the back with Teresa sat in it! Teresa's face was a picture. She remained deathly white and silent for the remainder of the journey. I think she was in shock!

Having explained that 'Mavis' looked like the PopeMobile, I must tell you about the time my good friends Mike and Tina Donovan were seeing me off from our regular Friday night Folk Night at the Tudor pub on Tudor Road, a colourful area of Cardiff. They were bending down talking to me through the window, when Tina was suddenly aware of a man staggering behind her with a hand fumbling in his pocket. "What do you want?" she barked. Much to our amusement, he very drunkenly replied, "Two hot dogs with plenty of onions, please."

'Mavis' served me faithfully for ten years. The question of cost? Well, yes, it was very expensive, but you cannot put a price on independence.

# 13.

# To Some Degree

*My Graduation Day, with the Lladro figurine
that has pride of place in the living room.*

The Thalidomide Trust organised another holiday for a group of us in the summer of 1982. This time, having terrorised the New World with our presence, they found an adapted bus to give us the Grand Tour of Europe.

Paris, Brussels, Luxembourg, a quick flit over the border into Germany and then back home by way of Amsterdam was a great experience, not only for the tourism but also for a great chance to mix yet again with my fellows in a holiday atmosphere. We were one big family, it seemed, brothers and sisters brought together by a similar misfortune. We travelled in a little world of our own and, for a couple of weeks, had the everyday inconvenience of our particular requirements taken care of without our having a single worry.

Refreshed and re-invigorated, I came home to find disappointment awaiting me.

My application to the University of Wales had been received, and I was called in for an interview with the head of the psychology department. Much excitement. But I had not been called in to discuss my academic qualifications for the place. It was to tell me that, because the university building was two storeys, there was no way in which they could accommodate someone who drove around in an electric wheelchair. Not only that, but they were not prepared to upset their set routine to help.

Accustomed as I was by now to having obstacles placed in my path, it was, I think, the bland dismissal that infuriated me so much.

I sat at home for few days fuming, feeling pretty sorry for myself. But then came an invitation to attend for an interview at Cardiff University. I thought of asking them, sarcastically, just how many floors they had before I bothered to show up but then thought better of it.

I met with not only the head of the department but also the dean, head of psychology, two lecturers from the psychology department, the university nurse and a representative from the student body. Much more impressive, and my 'problems' did not seem to overwhelm them. Indeed, they seemed eager to make it all work for me, something of a refreshing change after my previous experience.

Their attitude was totally different from UWIST's. They wanted to give me a place and wanted to know what I needed to make life easier. I could not believe my ears when they asked me questions about my interests, hobbies, qualifications and what I could do. We discussed and came up with innovative and often simple solutions to a few minor obstacles. They told me there and then that there was a place for me if I wanted it. If I wanted it?! Mum (who had driven me to the interview) and I went to the nearest off–licence and brought a bottle of Champagne.

I was accepted, awarded a place on my own merit and joined the other students to do a three-year degree course in psychology, just like any other girl.

Freshers week soon came around, and for practical reasons (not all of the university was wheelchair accessible), my wonderful Mum helped me get to all the places for signing on for courses, the library, the union and other places. For the first term (until I passed my driving test), she also drove me back and forth to university.

At lectures in the theatres, where I was given a desk in the front, I made many good friends who were only too glad to pair up with me for practicals. Much of the stimulating conversation and debate was done in the coffee bar, at friends house parties or, inevitably, in the pub since *in vino veritas*, or so we thought. Those three years were the most mentally stimulating, hardest working and fastest moving of my life. I had a good social life, but because it often took me longer to do things than it did others, I spent many evenings and late nights re-writing (typing) lecture notes, writing essays, preparing for tutorials and, when the finals soon came around, revising frantically. I will always be grateful to Debbie for her help with typing important essays and my thesis; to Denise for the endless cups of coffee, digestive biscuits and moral support; and to Mum and Dad for all their encouragement and practical support. I would not have succeeded without them.

Apart from a little practical help, my fellow students and friends rarely treated me any differently than anyone else. We socialised and studied well together. Amanda Engle and Dave White, together with a few other students and I, became a regular team for our practical assignments. In these, my fellow students, comrades and friends always ensured that I did my fair share and sometimes a little more. On one occasion, whilst carrying out an experiment on reaction time, they had me wired to a computer for three hours. During a lengthy behavioural experiment – teaching a rat to do tricks – our rat Ben bit my finger. In response to my cries of "Get this bloody rat off my finger. I can't afford to lose any more," the reply was, "You manage all right with four. Will one fewer make a difference?"

I gather my reaction time was assessed as being above par for the course.

Without making me an exception, lecturers also did what they could to assist me. A few weeks into the course, I realised that getting books and papers from the library was proving very difficult. So I put a proposition to the lecturers to borrow their copies of the books we needed to read for tutorials or lectures. Naturally, I took great care of them.

When it came to my finals, the decision of under which conditions I sat my exams was ultimately mine. Even though it meant more work for my lecturers and tutors, I sat my exams at the same times as my fellow students but in a separate room so I could dictate the answers on to tape. These were later transcribed by the person overseeing me and submitted, together with my tapes and any notes, diagrams or graphs I had made.

It was wonderfully cheering to find that I was now accepted without reserve into the student body, but it did not do much to alleviate the physical barriers involved. Cardiff University were farsighted enough not to put obstacles in my way, but the builders and planners of the complex certainly had. Most of my lectures were held in the Park Place tower block, which was accessible to me. However, some were held in the Law Building which was mostly inaccessible for a powered wheelchair and almost so for a manual one. Only by dint of much huffing and puffing on the part of my fellow students was I able to make it at all, and the result was that we were usually late for lectures. They were probably exhausted as well. Something had to be done.

The staff agreed, and, following a meeting with my tutor and the other lecturers, they, quite remarkably, re-shuffled their agenda to accommodate little old me. By swapping things around, I could now take all my lectures in one location. Marvellous.

Something they could do little to help me with was taking notes. Most lecturers disliked handing out copies of their own notes to students, and for some recording them was a real no-no. As I have mentioned, writing was not the easiest thing for me to accomplish, so I'll leave you to imagine the scene. Head down over the desk, cocked at a ridiculous angle to balance my pen between my two little fingers, scribbling away furiously and hoping fervently that I would be able to read the scribble afterwards.

Essay writing and similar stuff was marginally easier since the final result could be beaten out on a typewriter (computers were only just coming onto the scene). My sister Debbie, now a qualified secretary, sometimes felt sorry for me and rattled off essays and, at the end of year two, my Theses. A blessed relief.

By now I am sure that you know me well enough to appreciate that, hard as I was working, I was certainly not going to miss out on the fun things in life, one of which was boys.

A summer holiday, whilst staying at Haighmoor House in Jersey with my sister Denise for two weeks, included a bit of a fling with Ritchie from Liverpool, a long distance relationship that lasted for three years.

Although my studies kept me fully occupied, I felt that I needed to do something other than swot away. So in January 1985 I started to do voluntary work for the Samaritans. Considering that I was about to take my final exams, I am not sure that it was such a good idea, in retrospect. And, on actually reaching the examination hall, I felt that it probably had not been. I was convinced that failure was looming.

Results were out in July and were posted on two notice boards, one for those who had passed and one for those that had not. Unable to bear the ordeal alone, I recruited Debbie and Denise to come along for moral support and to stand by with their handkerchiefs for the inevitable flood of tears.

With a show of bravado, I steeled myself and cruised up to the failures board. I was still searching for my name on the list – I knew it had to be there somewhere – when the girls came back from the other board, whooping with delight. I had passed.

It was a great night in the local pub. Before going off to celebrate, I rang Mum and Dad who were anxiously awaiting the results at home. And true to form, by the time the girls and I returned home, Mum had clogged up the telephone exchange, ringing everyone with her very proud news.

The graduation ceremony was held shortly after the results were published, and with me dressed in mortarboard and gown, the Moriarty family proudly attended en masse. Just before leaving the house, they gave me a gift: a beautiful and very appropriate Lladro figurine of a girl in a graduation outfit, sitting on a chair. I asked when had they brought it, only to be informed, "Two years ago."

I was distressed "Two years ago! What if I had failed? Could you have got your money back?"

I felt very moved and emotional when Mum replied, "With your determination and the effort you have made to be successful, we knew you would not fail."

But Denise soon had us all in fits with her version of the truth, "If you had failed, Mum would have swapped it for the third shepherd to add to her Nativity collection, you would have been sent to the salt mines and the rest of the family would have emigrated."

My triumph was complete as I was wheeled along in front of the dais so that the dean could lean over and shake both my fingers whilst the other students had to climb onto the stage. At the time all of that seemed to be quite all right, probably because I was just so relieved and excited about the fact that I had actually got a university degree, which really was beyond my wildest dreams. However, with hindsight, I should have asked the university to build a ramp up to the stage or for all the other students to just file past the front of the stage whilst receiving their degrees. I feel pretty confident that had I asked the students to do so, I would have got their support.

But my degree was due not only to my hard work, but also to the farsightedness of the university in allowing and assisting me to study in spite of all the difficulties for us both. Particularly as I was the first disabled person who was a wheelchair user to actually start and complete a degree at the university.

# 14.

# Convincing the World

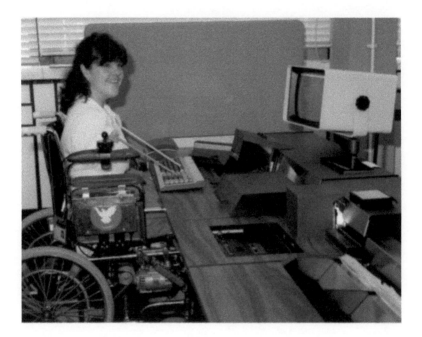

*Managing the Remittance processing system at Companies House.*

I am sure you will agree with me that one of the most depressing tasks in this world is the writing of job applications. For starters, you are pretty sure that none of your qualifications will be good enough for the job and convincing a cynical employer that they are is difficult enough for the sleekest looking girl around the block.

Doing it as a disabled person who is also a wheelchair user, and trying to make employers accept that you are the best person for the job, is the job seeking equivalent of a slog up the Eiger (North Face) with one hand tied behind your back. And so it proved to be. With much agonising labour, I handcrafted more than two hundred and fifty letters, of the begging variety, to various employers that I felt could use my talents.

We (in the UK) did not have the Disability Discrimination Act in those days, and – oops a daisy – accidentally or otherwise an application could fall off the desk into the bin. And more than three-quarters of companies didn't even have the decency to reply. Those few that did said something like this: 'Dear Rosie, nice to hear you've got a degree, pat on the head, well done, but we don't want to give you a bloody job, way too difficult.'

That was a shock to my system. It was almost as bad as being thrown out of the shops all those years earlier. I thought, 'Hang on a minute. I've got qualifications. I'm as worthy as you are. Why won't you give me a job?' And then I would get angry again.

I concluded, now being a psychologist with a bit of paper to prove it, that nearly all were in urgent need of my services since hardly any even bothered to reply.

But one did. And it looked ideal. Lansdowne Hospital, on the southern outskirts of Cardiff, did. They needed an information officer, just the sort of thing I was qualified for. With my long experience of actually being treated in hospitals, I was shoe-in for the job. Also, since it was a hospital, I envisaged absolutely no problems regarding access issues or attitudinal barriers.

I was wrong, horribly wrong.

Having attended the interview, which went well, I was then informed that the job was mine. While waiting for a date to start, I received a three-page letter from the administrators explaining why they would no longer give me the job. The primary excuse, tucked in amongst a lot of piffle, was that I would need assistance to go to the toilet. The fact that I had managed perfectly well during my time at college and beforehand shows just what a pathetic and specious excuse it was. In fact, we had rather anticipated that such a thing might come into question, and so my Mother had arranged to be on hand to take care of the matter. Lansdowne Hospital need have had no concerns on that score, besides which I had addressed this matter at the interview.

I was devastated. First came the shock of such an unfair rejection and then anger at the thoughtlessness of those who had first offered and then taken away the hope. I felt that it was unimaginably cruel, and, until then (apart from being force-fed cabbage), I had never been treated so abominably by anyone.

For days on end I sobbed, unable to reconcile myself to the disappointment after I had worked so hard. Had it all been a waste of time and effort?

Over the previous years, I had been buoyed up and sustained by the support of those around me. Even the rejection by the University of Wales had been tempered with a certain degree of common sense in their decision, even if they had expressed it badly. But I was stunned by the sheer duplicity of the hospital in first offering me the job and then withdrawing it.

While I was still reeling from the disappointment, another letter arrived, this time from a civil service department. Companies House wrote and invited me along for an interview. It struck me that, apart from hardly needing the services of a qualified psychologist, Companies House would be even less favourably inclined towards me than would a hospital. So it was without much hope, following the last debacle, that I wheeled myself along for the interview.

To my astonishment there seemed to be no stigma attached to my position, and indeed, the people I interviewing me, seemed more than a little interested. This may have been because that, now getting somewhat desperate in terms of wanting a job, I offered to work for them for one month, without pay, so that I could prove that I could do the job!

At the interview I had to demonstrate my ability to take notes, answer the telephone and use the keyboard on the newly installed computers that the office were now using. The latter I accomplished by using a couple of dowling rods, wooden sticks rather like sawn-off billiard cues. This performance fascinated them, and I was asked back on two more occasions to repeat the exercise for other staff members. It made me feel a bit like a performing dog in a circus, but I suppose the idea was to make quite sure that I would not find myself out of my depth should they hire me.

The culmination was that I had to demonstrate my ability to be able to wheel myself around the open-plan office, visiting each workstation in turn. On the face of it, this would have seemed to have been a perfectly sensible precaution to ensure that I would be able to cope. Subsequently, I was told that it was, in fact, to ensure that none of the staff would feel uncomfortable with my presence. To their eternal credit, none did, and I became an executive officer in Companies House. It was, indeed, a middle management job and some recompense for all the effort I had made to obtain my degree, if not exactly the sort of job I had envisaged.

Civil servants in general are never thought to be blessed with either imagination or much thought for their fellows, but at Companies House they proved to be outstanding exceptions to the rule. Incredibly, they overcame for me the major obstacle that the hospital had put in my way. They offered my Mother a job in a different department, but in the same building, so that she could be around to take care of matters that I could not manage for myself – the loo.

It was an amazing example of thoughtfulness and alone did much to restore my faith in the goodness of those around me, a faith that had been badly dented by the actions of Lansdowne Hospital. Mum had been considering taking a part-time job at a florists but, as always, put my needs first and the Moriarty double act became a fixture in the office.

Having a job and an income for the first time brought mixed emotions with it as part of the baggage. An upsurge of confidence, undoubtedly, for here was proof that I could make my own way in the world. At the same time, because I was still dependent upon my family for many things instilled in me a lingering fear. One day, I knew, I would wake up and find them gone. And then how would I manage? The thought of being suddenly thrust into the care of perfect strangers frightened me to death.

My mixture of achievement and uncertainty must have affected my personal relationships too, for after a summer holiday in Yugoslavia with Ritchie, followed by a weekend at his home in Liverpool, he told me that it was all over. Undoubtedly I was upset although Mum and Denise thought it was for the best, as they had never thought we were matched for each other anyway. However, being dumped on the platform of Liverpool Station is a bit of a blow to any girl's ego.

But it may have made my next life-changing decision easier.

I decided to flee the coop.

# 15.

# Going Solo

*Mum, Dad, cousin Mary (left), Rosie and Denise celebrating completion day for my bungalow in September 1987.*

Now with a secure job, I was ready to put an end to the insecurity that was troubling me. My fear was of losing, perhaps almost overnight, the support of my family who had done so much to take care of me and were experts in my particular personal and physical requirements. Mentally, I felt that there was no challenge I could not now meet but physically was a different matter. However I tried, I had to come to the realisation that I could never be totally independent of others. But, of course, living independently does not necessarily mean living alone.

Rather than postponing the evil day when I would be thrust, willy-nilly, into having to accept the help of total strangers, I decided to pre-empt the matter. I would go and live on my own, using professional people to do the job Mum and Dad had performed so wonderfully for me over the years.

Explaining this to them would have been an almost impossible task had they been just ordinary parents. But, as you have seen from my history so far, they were extraordinary parents.

Although they protested initially, once I explained to them my fears and aspirations, they understood. We discussed and debated the pros and cons endlessly, as with all important matters that any of our family were going to undertake. It was not going to be easy. I did not want to put myself into a situation where I was either vulnerable or setting myself up for failure. If anything happened to either of them and I was still living at home, the burden of looking after me 24/7, I felt, would have been too great for the other to cope with. I did not want to end up in a residential home or still be living at home with strangers all of a sudden having to see to my needs and requirements.

Furthermore, like all young women in their early twenties, I just wanted independence, freedom and to make my own choices, even if that meant making mistakes, but being allowed to learn from those mistakes. I also felt that because my parents, particularly, had devoted so much of their lifetime to looking after me, now was the right time for me to make the move. They were still young and, consequently, should have been in a situation where, if they wanted to go out for a night, they did not have to worry about who was going to look after me. If they wanted to go away on holidays, they could just do so off the cuff and again not worry about who was going to look after me. In my eyes they deserved that. Besides, I had no intentions of moving to Mars, just a couple of miles and a phone call away.

So after much debate and discussion, far from being upset at my decision, they applauded it and, as self- sacrificing as ever, went out of their way to help me to accomplish my goal of independence.

The first item on the agenda was, of course, to find a bungalow that could be adapted for me. We had a riot. Our house was flooded with specifications of likely properties, and, as with most house hunters, the choices seemed endless. We trekked around the area viewing bungalows vaguely suitable, unsuitable and totally out of the question, having fun doing it. The various pros and cons were argued over endlessly and sometimes heatedly. Everyone had an opinion, and the search could have gone on forever had we let it.

I wound up buying the very first one we had viewed. It was wonderful and just what I had always been looking for.

Now we tackled what we thought would be the simple part of the equation. Finding a personal assistant for me, or, as eventually advertised, 'A Helper for Rosie'. In our innocence we thought a phone call to social services would result in an avalanche of offers, but this was not to be the case. For nearly two years, we waited for Cardiff Social Services to come up with a care package that we could all agree on. Mr Micawber had nothing on us. Hope sprang eternal, and we knew that, eventually, something or someone had to turn up.

Meanwhile, there was much to be done. The property had to be purchased and a grant obtained for the alterations that would be needed to turn it into a 'Rosie House'. The bedroom and bathroom both needed to be enlarged, and all the light switches and power sockets had to be re-positioned so that I could reach them. An automatic door system was installed so that I could roll in and out without difficulty. Those who complain about the costs of remodelling their homes will sympathise with all this. Explaining these requirements to the average contractor is not an easy matter. And then there is the little matter of paying for it.

The alterations to the bungalow, which would mean an alteration to my lifestyle, were accompanied by a less planned change as well.

Back in the 1960s, when the campaign for compensation was in full flow, parents across the United Kingdom had formed the Thalidomide Society.

The society held many meetings, some national and some regional. At one of these regional get-togethers in Cardiff, I had met up with my first secret admirer from the limb fitting rendezvous, Stephen.

We had kept in touch for many years as friends, fairly regular phone calls, the odd letter, an occasional night out. And now, just when I was in the throes of purchasing my bungalow, out of the blue came a phone call. Would I care to accompany him to the opening of a new restaurant? Stephen was by now a qualified Solicitor and, having done work for the establishment, had been invited to its inaugural beanfeast. Diligent readers of my story will have gathered that Rosie was never one to turn down a social event if the opportunity arose.

It turned out to be more than just a wonderful evening. Stephen confessed that he had been secretly in love with me for years but had been afraid to mention it lest he spoil the friendship.

For my part I basked in the glow and kept casting sly glances. "He's a good looking fellow – and charming with it. Could do a lot worse."

Next thing I knew, we were engaged. Which just goes to show what a bit of limb fitting will do for a girl.

# 16.

# A New Life

*Here comes the Bride… and a proud Dad!*

*For better or worse, and things have got better and better.*

*Smiles all round. She's off our hands at last!!*

129

By 1988 the decade of the '80s was fading away and with it memories of the scandal of the Thalidomide affair were fading also.

Writing about disabled children is an emotive subject and makes for what Fleet Street refers to as "good copy." Writing about disabled adults is merely an unfortunate and embarrassing occurrence and, unless coupled with a newsworthy event, rarely surfaces in the media.

And by now we were all adults. The shock and horror that had greeted our appearance on the world stage had now been assuaged by the chequebook of Distillers. Blood money had exonerated them from any culpability of involvement that would, under different circumstances, have been construed as being criminally negligent. For not only were so many of us left to face a difficult existence, many others had failed to survive at all. It had been mass murder, legally condoned by government and big business.

Now the dues had been paid, justice had been seen to have been done in the eyes of the public and our stories were relegated to the minor pages, when they appeared at all. By now not only was I feeling my independence but I was busily involved in becoming even more so, for my bungalow was now available.

My truly independent life was just beginning.

I started to get the bungalow together and sorted out to meet my needs to live independently of my family. As you may imagine, it was a horrendously busy time for me. I had a full-time job and a very busy social life. One of my social activities was singing. I used to have quite a nice singing voice and would confidently sing in public. Quite often I would be asked to sing at family and friends weddings. I sang the 'Ave Maria' at my sister Debbie's wedding when she married José. The irony there was that José used to tease me incessantly about my singing. (He teases everybody and anybody once he finds out what their Achilles' heel is.) Deep down though I think he secretly enjoyed listening to me!

Usually a couple of times a week I would go to folk clubs with my good friends Mike and Tina Donovan. Mike and Gerry Nash would sing primarily, and I would do a little session at some stage during the night. Sometimes we would sing at St Peter's social club with Frank Hennessy.

I met Mike and Tina through Mike's sister Gail, who had been one of the helpers on the first Thalidomide Trust organised holiday that I went on. We hit it off immediately, and after the holiday, when she visited her family in Cardiff, we got together, and she introduced me to Mike and Tina, who have been firm friends since 1980. I was a bridesmaid at their wedding. I am godmother to their daughter Kerry, and Tina was one of my matrons of honour. By now my social life had taken a new and not totally expected turn.

Following my dinner date with him in May 1987, Stephen and I began to date.

We had known each other nearly all of our lives, so the possibility of marrying one's best friend seemed not totally out of the question. We seemed to be totally compatible, and the pleasure we derived from each other's company was obvious to all and sundry.

Four months into our relationship, Stephen proposed – and, naturally, I accepted. We had known each other so long that there seemed to be little point in postponing the wedding, and my family flung themselves into the organising with a vengeance. It looked like everybody in the whole wide world was happy about the forthcoming marriage – except Stephen's parents. We could not understand what the problem could be since his parents had known me throughout my childhood and that Stephen and I were longtime friends. We little thought there would be any opposition to the match, especially from them. Stephen's parents have never said why they were so opposed to the match, but his grandmother did say that even if Stephen had brought home Diana Spencer, his mother would not have approved of her for her son.

I suspected that they may have had issues with our having or not having children. If that were the case, it would have been better to say so rather than make our lives miserable at a time that was supposed to be a very happy time. Sadly, we did not even know if they would attend the wedding, not until the day itself, when Stephen was in the foyer of the church greeting our guests. But things have turned out better. They became wonderful grandparents. But they missed out on the excitement of planning their son's wedding: which church, the reception, the colour scheme, the bridesmaids, the best man, the honeymoon and all the other bits and pieces that make up such a special day. My family and I carried the entire load, and I have to say that we probably preferred it that way.

My beloved Nana Cummins had died earlier in the year, which was a great loss to all of us but especially to Mum and me. From the moment my Mother became pregnant, Nana was always there to support her. From the moment I was born, she was always there to support, advise and encourage me. She was delighted when Stephen and I got engaged, for she adored him. Although she did not live to see us actually married, she did enjoy being involved with the planning of our wedding.

We planned everything down to the finest detail. Well, everything bar one – the weather. For on the great day, the heavens opened, not just for an odd shower or two, but for a deluge that would have impressed Noah and made him hurry up with his Ark.

For obvious reasons all the functions had to be in accessible places. We decided upon St Peter's Church, as St Peter's had been there for me throughout my life. My parents were married there. My christening, communion and confirmation were there. It seemed inevitable that I would be married there.

We had a full nuptial mass, with folk singers (many of whom were friends) and a choir (primarily made up from the St Joseph's Mothers Union (Mum was president). The church was packed to the rafters with family and friends from all around the world.

At the ceremony there were two priests, one a family friend, Father Alan Hale, the other our parish priest, Father Philip Scanlon; two altar boys, my cousins John and Paul Moriarty; two ushers, my cousins Dermot and Patrick Cowman; and three bridesmaids, my two sisters and Tina. Well, technically, because Debbie and Tina were married, they were matrons of honour. Denise gave herself the title of chief bridesmaid. We did not argue with that. Guy Phillips,

Stephen's best man, was a friend from his university days. Hundreds of family and friends together with well-wishers, including casual passers-by joined in congratulating us.

There must have been some string pulling done at the Vatican, for at the end of the ceremony, we received a papal blessing, a great honour, all the more so since Stephen is not a Catholic.

The whole affair went off without a hitch. We had planned everything down to the last buttonhole flower. But, as I said, the weather refused to cooperate. It rained buckets, cats and dogs. This only impeded the photo shoots which we had planned for outdoors. We merely moved them inside.

The best part was that Stephen was there, and Rosie was there, and we were very happy.

I think that in the end his mother was glad that he had not brought Diana home; at least, I like to think so.

The reception in St Peter's Church Hall was one big party. Dad's speech was very moving and emotional. He talked of our relationship being a match made in heaven. Stephen's speech included his demonstrating that he was bestowing all his worldly goods upon me. He produced a battered old cardboard box, inscribed 'Worldly Goods'. I believe it was empty, but nothing mattered to me on that day. My sisters and Auntie Nancy wrote and recited poems about us. The atmosphere was electric, and I wanted it to last forever. However, Steve's biggest problem was dragging me away from the fun so that we could get off on our honeymoon in Paris.

You may be interested to know that there have been about twenty-four Thalidomide-impaired people who have sought the company of each other, thus culminating in twelve Thalidomide-impaired couples in the United Kingdom. And of the rest of the Thalidomide-impaired people who have sought relationships, they have generally been with other non-disabled people.

We set up house in the bungalow. I had already been working on it and had moved in a month before the wedding to get used to my new Personal Assistants and being independent, no longer relying too heavily upon my immediate family. Stephen and his best man stayed there the night before the wedding while I stayed with my family for a bit of a hen party. Upon our return from the honeymoon, we moved into what was now our bungalow, with my PAs coming to assist me first thing in the morning and then returning in the evening for a couple of hours. At that time I was working full time in one direction of Cardiff at Companies House, and Stephen was working full time in the other direction as a partner in a firm of solicitors in Porthcawl, a situation that continued until 1993.

# 17.

# Plans, Hopes and Grief

*The last photograph I have of my beautiful Mum, 6 February 1992.*

After the excitement of the wedding, we settled down to a comfortable domestic routine. Feeling that my artificial limbs were neither useful nor ornamental, I now dispensed with them. Years later Stephen found them in the attic, still with the garter attached.

In 1990 Mum and I took part in a documentary called *Tin Lids* to celebrate our thirty years' anniversary. I am quoted as saying:

"In about sixty years time, Thalidomide people will be extinct. We will go down in the history books as a generation of people that will, or at least should, never appear again. We are just a blip in the history of mankind."

And yet to our horror we learned that the drug Thalidomide was still being used. In fact, although used for research purposes only and allegedly given only to named patients, its use was increasing at an alarming rate. All the while we and our parents had believed that when Thalidomide was withdrawn from use on 2 December 1961, it would never be used again. Now, however, there was an accident out there waiting to happen.

I would never have imagined that less than three years after making that statement the First Tuesday team (Yorkshire Television, 1 June 1993) would produce a shocking documentary. Screened across the UK, it showed the horrifying scenes of young children twenty years my junior displaying the same characteristic limb deformities which caused a worldwide outcry when the Thalidomide scandal broke many years previously.

First Tuesday found in Brazil alone twenty-one new cases of Thalidomide, aged from four to twenty-three, in such diverse locations as Rio de Janeiro and the heart of the Amazon jungle. A further five had reportedly died, and nine women had had abortions because their babies were affected by Thalidomide. The UK-based charity Thalidomide Children of Brazil found fifty-five new cases of Thalidomide in Brazil, aged from two to fifteen. How many more cases worldwide have been suppressed?

Thalidomide is given to people with leprosy throughout Brazil. It does not cure or treat the leprosy itself but is given to treat leprosy-reaction, a side effect, as a result of the powerful antibiotics which are given to treat the leprosy.

After the second-generation story broke, a couple from Bournemouth, Helen and Gerry Alford, were so shocked by what they had seen on television that they decided to take positive action to help the children in Brazil. Helen, herself a full-time wheelchair user, started a campaign that was to have a far-reaching effect throughout the United Kingdom. With her tireless campaigning, Helen was able to raise enough money to enable her and Gerry to travel to Brazil on numerous occasions, taking supplies of wheelchairs and artificial limbs to help relieve some of the devastating consequences for the new generation of children that aroused as much emotion as when the first generation of children were born.

In addition to taking supplies out to Brazil, Helen also brought children over to Britain and arranged for them to be fitted with various types of prosthesis. One such child was a girl named Rafaela. By this time Helen had been to the Thalidomide Society conferences to highlight the work she was doing with the Brazilian children, and we invited her to come to Cardiff with Rafaela and her mother to see how Steve and I managed. So, on a trip to Britain to be fitted with cosmetic ears, Rafaela and her mother travelled to South Wales with Helen and Gerry to see us.

Rafaela had been born without ears and slightly impaired hands. She was about twelve years old when we met her and was becoming increasingly conscious of her appearance. So much so that she would only wear her hair down and to cover the tiny flaps of skin that were visible where her ears should have been. We were unable to speak a word of Portuguese; likewise, neither Rafaela nor her mother could speak English. However, the bond which transcends all Thalidomide children was evident on this day also. We had tea and enjoyed a wonderful Sunday afternoon together. James enjoyed playing with Rafaela, as much I think as she enjoyed mothering him. When it was time for them to leave, we waved good-bye with a genuine hope that Rafaela would do well when she returned to Brazil.

Rafaela will be a young women now, and I often find myself wondering what became of the little girl who we had the pleasure of inviting into our home. I just hope that she was able to gain a little encouragement and confidence from seeing what we were able to do.

Shortly after Rafaela's visit, the Alfords had to give up their campaigning work due to ill health. But the baton of campaigning for these children had been passed to Brian Gault, himself a Thalidomide-impaired man born without arms.

This period was a turning point for me in terms of researching and writing about Thalidomide. However, other events would happen in my life before I got to this stage.

Although paper shuffling in a civil service office was not what I had had in mind for a career, it was a pleasant environment, and the rest of the staff did much to heal the bruises I had suffered whilst looking for work.

And, of course, I was still in close contact with my family, my Mother being there for me daily.

I suppose I should have been content with the status quo, but, contrary to the opinion of many, being a little different in shape does not mean that your feelings are in any way different from anyone else's. And we wanted what most young couples wanted. We wanted to have a child.

Sometimes I think that many people forget that, although to them I may look a bit odd, most of the hidden parts work in exactly the same way as in anyone else.

I always remember a well-meaning nurse at the Nuffield Orthopaedic Hospital, Oxford, when I was thirteen or fourteen years old taking Bev and me to one side and explaining the 'facts of life' to us. As we were probably more aware of these than she was, how we managed to stifle our giggles I will never know. It was all a bit embarrassing both for her and for us.

What I did not appreciate at the time was that she was trying to tell us that the medical profession had no knowledge of our future medical expectations or requirements. She could not confirm whether we would even menstruate or be able to conceive or, indeed, how on earth we would be able to have sexual relationships. I am delighted to tell you that most of us Thalidomide girls have been successful on all three counts!

By this time I had done a good deal of research on the subject of Thalidomide and its effects and was pretty convinced that any of the impairments that we had as a direct result of the drug were not hereditary in character. But whilst there was to be no problem on that score, actually conceiving proved not to be as easy as we hoped. In 1991 my first conception ended in failure when I had my first miscarriage at eight weeks.

The doctors at the fertility centre whom we consulted were not the most encouraging.

"Are you sure? How will you manage? Your health may be affected, you know."

Talk like that merely made me more determined. I tried a mild fertility drug, with no result.

We were disappointed. But, then, we were both inured to disappointment, and the only thing to do was to keep trying.

Apart from a lack of a wanted pregnancy, 1992 started out to be a wonderful year. But as so often in this life, just when it seemed nothing could mar our happiness, tragedy struck.

In February Mum and Dad were leaving for a well-earned holiday in Tenerife. On the eighth they called in to say good-bye as they were on their way to a party. After I had waved them good-bye, I closed the front door and cried. I had no idea why and felt stupid for doing so. Four days later we received the call. Mum had died of a heart attack.

It had been Dad's birthday, and she had done some shopping in the morning, preparing a surprise birthday party for him. Joining him and their friends at the pool, she had taken a short dip and settled down on a sun- lounger to read the book I had loaned her, *A Circle of Friends*, by Maeve Binchy.

Suddenly she had trouble breathing. Because Mum had asthma, it was assumed that it was another attack, but this time it seemed to be something more serious. Dad tried mouth to mouth resuscitation without success. By chance four qualified nurses were present. But nothing could be done.

My much beloved mother died at the age of forty-nine years.

Miles away, we were unable to say good-bye properly, nor could we comfort my father, and so the grieving never ends.

Nothing prepares you for the loss of a loved one. Particularly when that loved one is still so young and when it is unexpected.

Over the years I have lost many people with whom I had a close relationship or who had a great influence on my life: my grandparents, in particular Nana Cummins, who had been like a second mother to me, was another very special lady who was always there either for me or for my Mum); Uncle Peter; my good friends Beverley and Janette; but none more so than my Mum.

Mum was not just my Mum; she was my best friend, my confidant, the primary person who looked after me, my rock. She was selfless in her devotion to me, always encouraged me to be independent and always told me how proud she was of me.

One of the things that breaks my heart is that my Mother always carried with her the guilt of having taken Thalidomide in the first place. We discussed this occasionally, but no matter how many times I told her that it was not her fault, that I never blamed her or held her accountable, I would know that she was hurting. Similarly, I know that Dad sometimes feels the same way too, but, regrettably, he is not keen on deep or emotional discussions, so it is not a conversation to be taken too far.

Thankfully, we have always been a touchy-feely family and often say I love you to each other. Also that special hug or kiss would convey what the other one was trying to say.

There is a song that I used to sing to my Mum, which I also sang to James to get him off to sleep as a baby:

**M**. is for the memories you gave me.
**O**. is for the oaths you made to keep.
**T**. is for the tears you shed to bear me, and
**H**. is for your heart, your heart of gold.
**E**. is for your eyes they shine like diamonds, and
**R**. is for the rights and rights to be.
Put them all together, you get mother, and mother means the whole wide world to me.

What a huge impact fate can have on our lives! Only four years previously I had moved out of the family home to become more independent and less reliant on my family and so that my parents at long last could have more of a life of their own. My biggest fear had been of losing one of them whilst I would still be living at home. Although I was by now happily married and living in my own home, I never imagined that I would lose one of my parents so young and so soon.

I still carry with me the guilt that, inadvertently, the extra stresses and strains of bringing me up may have taken their toll on my mother's health. It is impossible to put into words how much I miss her and hate the fact that things could never be the same. Part of me died that day. A link in the chain that had bound us together for so many years was no more.

People tell you that time is a good healer. Well, that is not true I'm afraid. All that happens is that over a period of time you become more accustomed to the situation, and whether you like it or not, life has to go on.

In June of that year, I thought I was pregnant once more. The first test was inconclusive, and we spent an uneasy time until the second proved positive.

We were guardedly optimistic, but on a holiday in Scotland, I began to experience some premature cramps and pains. Once more I was to miscarry. With all the progress in medical science, doctors were unable to tell us the reason for the miscarriages. And each time we were heartbroken.

More disappointment. By this time my civil service job was not giving me the personal satisfaction that I was seeking. Later that year I decided to make a break and find something that my talents were better suited for. A chance to take voluntary redundancy came up, and I jumped at the opportunity, leaving the service on 12 March 1993.

By the time of my third miscarriage, we thought that we were fated never to have children of our own and started to consider adoption. Sadly, adoption agencies were not interested in disabled people as parents, even though we felt we would have made as good, and more likely better, parents than more than half their applicants. Rebuffed, we were just at the stage of possibly going for in vitro fertilisation treatment, but before we had a chance for in-depth discussions on the topic, voila, a miracle: I conceived yet again.

Mum always knew how desperately I would have loved a child of my own and always said that if it were meant to happen, it would. However, during a conversation with my sisters about having a child, I was taken aback by their reactions. It was along the same lines as some members of the medical profession. "Are you sure? How will you manage? Your health may be affected, you know."

So this time we didn't tell anyone for fear of jinxing things and waited until I was past the three-month stage of pregnancy, fingers crossed. About then we were invited, along with the rest of the family, to my Auntie Nancy's home for Sunday lunch. It was the anniversary of our grandparents' death, so there had been a big mass. As all the family were gathered together, we thought it would be a good time to give the news so that if it was too big a surprise, they would be there to console each other. My Dad nearly passed out with shock, and my sisters too, but everyone quickly composed themselves and expressed their congratulations. In anticipation of the hoped for reaction, we had brought along some pink Champagne to celebrate. And celebrate we did. This time we just knew all would be well.

As do many pregnant women, I blossomed, bloomed and ballooned during the pregnancy, but because of my previous losses, I didn't want any of the intrusive tests that are given to find out if the child has Downs syndrome or any number of other impairments. I accepted only scans. If we were blessed with a child, disabled or not, it would be pure destiny and, remembering my own childhood, would not have been an issue. I was sure that the Thalidomide strain was not passed genetically and therefore would not affect any of my births.

And I was right. As you know, James was perfectly wonderful.

# 18.

# A New Life and a New Job

*At the helm of the 'enterprise' preparing for the next workshop.*

On leaving the civil service, I cast about me for a calling that would fit both my talents and, perhaps as important, my particular requirements.

Boring though it may have been, except for the many good friends that I had made whilst at Companies House, my years in the office had also done a good deal for my self-esteem, and I now felt ready to take on the world.

I took a correspondence course in journalism and writing and started to write my autobiography. (Yes, the one you're reading now. It was a long gestation!) I had always promised my Mother that I would write a book, even if it just got to be a manuscript for the family to enjoy. Every New Year's resolution would be, "This year I'm going to start that book," but every year my time came to be occupied with doing something else.

Voluntary work with organisations working with and for disabled people started to absorb more and more of my attention.

Disabled people and their organisations were getting more and more politically motivated and wanted to have some form of anti-discrimination legislation passed through Parliament. I became a member of the Cardiff and Vale Coalition of Disabled People and recall with pride the first time that we travelled to London for a demonstration at Trafalgar Square seeking civil rights legislation for disabled people. It was very empowering.

One of the images from the demonstration that will remain with me forever was of looking behind me whilst at the tail end of a huge group of disabled people who had decided to bring Whitehall to a standstill — and, I saw a homeless man who didn't have any legs, he was using two skateboards tied together for a makeshift wheelchair. He had turned around and was holding his hand up in the air. Just behind him were three double-decker buses that had pulled up beside each other to help us bring the traffic to a standstill. It looked as if he alone had single-handedly accomplished this. I so wish that I had had a camera with me that day.

For two years I also did some broadcasting with Touch AM on the *Contact* programme. It dawned upon me that here might be the outlet that I was looking for.

I enrolled on one of the first Disability Equality Training courses for disabled trainers, which was held at Stakpole in West Wales. From this I gleaned a better understanding of the Social Model of Disability. In this model, people with impairments are seen as disabled by their environment, the attitudes of others and the policies, practices and procedures of organisations. Not much can be done to change impairments. However, a great deal can be done to get rid of barriers and create a more equal society in all aspects of life. I thought, 'Yes, I can relate to this. I really understand all of this.' Learning about the Social Model of Disability was like being enlightened; something you have always known, but did not know it had a name. I already had a lot of training skills through the civil service, and having been a manager, I had skills in training other people, so I thought I could marry the two and I started leading Disability Equality Training myself. Things kicked off, and by

1995 I was being asked to do so much training I decided to set this up as a business, to give it more kudos. All those years of doing business studies paid off at last.

Many women, when they are pregnant, develop strange cravings, banana-and-peanut butter sandwiches and similar exotic tastes. Me, I developed a craving to go into business.

I suppose that these days it would be referred to as multi-tasking. Preparing for a baby would have kept most people busy, and for Stephen and me, both born Thalidomide-impaired, it was especially challenging.

We had already achieved so much. We were both well educated, loved by our families, had learned to drive, found good jobs, got married, and now here was I preparing to run my own business – and preparing for an addition to our family. We had a lovely home and a busy social life. Bringing up a child was surely going to be a doddle after all that.

If anybody frowned on our decision to have a child, well, we would just prove them wrong.

I must have been born Mother Earth, and I think under other circumstances I would have had lots of children. Throughout my pregnancy I blossomed and, naturally, got wider! Obviously, I got more tired as the pregnancy wore on and, consequently, had to do things like getting on and off the toilet and in and out of bed more slowly and cautiously.

The reaction of family and friends and even casual acquaintances to our impending family were many and varied. Shocked, surprised, curious and, fortunately, more often than not, pleased. But the questions were legion.

"How did you get pregnant?"

"Err, well, if you don't know by now."

"I guess you will have to stay in bed for the whole nine months?"

"I certainly hope not. I have got a business to run."

"What about your health?"

"I'm pregnant, not ill."

And the most stupid one of all, we thought: "Who will look after the baby?"

We had all the answers. After all, we had had a long time to think about it during the years of disappointment. We watched how other people cared for their children and worked out exactly how we would manage at every stage. What gadgets, equipment or physical support from others we might need. The various devices we might need to invent, adapt or purchase. Most people look at salad tongs and think of them only for serving salad. A disabled person can see a myriad of other uses, for example, in gathering up building blocks and other small toys. As they say, 'necessity is the mother of invention'.

My business was flourishing, and I worked right up until two weeks before James was born.

At that time, during the particularly hot summer we were having, I announced to the class I was holding that it might be a good idea if they brushed up on their obstetrics as I was due to drop any moment. I could imagine them stampeding to the exit doors, but they all put on cool exteriors and stayed. After that, I went into graceful retirement from work until the great day arrived.

Then, punctual to the day, after I had waddled onto the toilet at 8.00 a.m. on 9 August 1995, my waters broke. I remember thinking, 'Gosh, it's a good job it happened now. If I'd been in my electric wheel chair we could have had a nasty short circuit.'

On 15 October 1995, James was christened at St Peter's. Afterwards we held a celebration in the church hall with lots of high jinks with family and friends.

A couple of months later I attended my first United International Thalidomiders (UNITH) conference in Germany. Although I had got to know many Thalidomide-impaired people over the years from the UK, it was an interesting experience to also meet Thalidomide-impaired people from other parts of the world. I had always been aware that no matter where or under which circumstances I have met other Thalidomide-impaired people, we have instantly warmed to each other. It is almost as if we are like brothers and sisters; there is certainly a bond between us. Perhaps it was having a commonality of knowing what one specific thing caused our unique situation.

I have to acknowledge that not all Thalidomide-impaired people feel this way. Indeed, some of them have gone to extraordinary lengths to disassociate themselves from the Thalidomide group. My personal view is that perhaps they are not comfortable with their impairments; consequently, coming face to face with somebody who might look almost identical to them would be more than they could bear. That must be quite a distressing situation to be in because, in reality, mixing with other Thalidomide-impaired people has great advantages. We can share information, discuss which gadgets and gizmos have worked for us, talk about and compare each other's medical conditions and experiences and have a lot of fun meeting people from all walks of life.

One thing we all have in common though, is our Thalidomide birthmark! Apart from our own natural birthmarks, all Thalidomide-impaired people have a red blemish or streak down the middle of our faces. This goes upwards in a V shape between our eyebrows. It was far more prevalent when we were babies and young children. But even now, if we get hot and bothered, you can see it on our faces.

I'll give you an insight into James's current sense of humour. Whilst I was trying to explain all this to him one day recently, he was listening to what I had to say in a somewhat bemused manner. Then came the grin and that mischievous twinkle in his eyes, "Oh, I get it. What you are trying to say mum is that you are all aliens from the planet Flid." Cheeky little monkey!

# 19.

# It's a Family Business

*James on his Christening Day, 15 October 1995,*
*wearing a family heirloom, my christening robe.*

*And with Mum and Dad.*

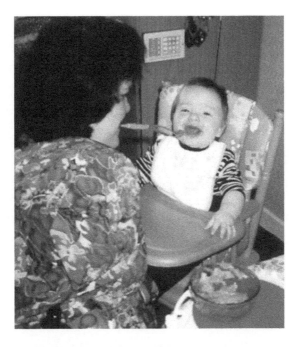

*Please, Mum, can I have some more!*

*Out and about with Mum travelling in style.*

We soon settled into the routine of feeding, winding, bathing, changing, playing, cuddling, sleeping. The only thing I could not do for James but could supervise was to bathe him. The one thing I chose to delegate, was changing dirty nappies. Having only two fingers from the shoulders means my face was just a little too close to the nappy for comfort!

We were well organised; we had thought and planned everything through in advance. For example, we bought a cot that had one side that went right down to the floor for easy access to James. We had a nappy changing unit made to our requirements; a car seat times two, one for my car, one for Steve's; a dozen bottles, long thin ones, or the Nipper Gripper type, which I found easier to handle. We would make up six bottles at a time, and the others would be sterilizing ready to be made up the next evening. Two of the most useful pieces of equipment were a portable baby seat, which we strapped on to the dining room chair so that James could sit at the table with us wherever we were and in which I could initially feed him until he was able to feed himself. The second useful piece of equipment was a backpack baby carrier, the kind that athletic parents use to carry their babies on their backs. I strapped this to the back of my electric wheelchair. James was then strapped into the backpack, and everybody was happy, particularly James because he could see where we were going, and when he was tired, he could fall asleep on my shoulder.

When I bottle fed him, I laid him flat on the dining room table. When he was on solids and in a high chair, I sellotaped two long plastic spoons together to make one long one, I would put the handle end in my mouth, scoop up the food and put it in James's mouth.

We employed a 'mother's help' (nicknamed 'Auntie Anne') a couple of days a week to help me look after James when Stephen was at work. I had used voice control to stop James harming himself while crawling and walking, but could not guarantee that this would work when we were out walking. So I bought some reins for him, only to discover that the strap was not long enough. Then I had the bright idea of attaching a retractable dog lead to the rein's strap. This allowed James enough freedom, and I had the security of knowing that I still had control.

The only downside to this was that there were actually members of the public who said things like, "Oh how cute. Is he pulling you along?" and, "He's a strong little chappy to be able to pull you along like that!" If I had a pound for everybody who said that or something else equally outrageous, I would be a rich woman now.

My stock answer, through gritted teeth and a false smile, was "Yes, it's a new Winter Olympics sport, babies pulling sledges through the snow, and I'm training him up!" It was usually worth it just to see their expressions.

However, there was one comment that really used to rile me, and that was, "I bet he is your arms and legs." No, absolutely not. He was not put on this earth to be my slave, and other people even thinking or implying that makes me so angry. I am vehemently against children being expected to look after their disabled parents. Don't get me wrong, making their bed, tidying away toys, helping to lay the table should be expected of children in every household. But expecting children to lift, dress, toilet, bathe, feed and give twenty-four-hour support to a disabled parent is, in my opinion, wholly wrong and unfair to the child.

It is absolutely essential that if there is a disabled person in a family, and that disabled person particularly needs personal support and assistance, then it must come from outside sources. By that I mean, disabled people must be supported and encouraged to employ Personal Assistants to help them with their everyday individual requirements. The funding to enable disabled people to do this must come from the local authorities. If disabled people are denied these opportunities, there is potential for there to be a breakdown in the family relationships, be that between the disabled person and her or his children or the disabled person and her or his partner.

Generally, when James was a baby and then as a toddler and now as a typical teenager, when we are out and about as a family, the reaction of members of the public is warm and positive. It can range from total indifference to quizzical curiosity, and James handles this in a polite and mature way.

Occasionally, if people stare, James has been known to pull a face at them, and if people ask him probing questions, he has been known to come back with an equally outrageous answer. For example, once when asked why his mum didn't have any arms or legs? He answered, "She fell into the lion's cage!"

James and I have a wonderful mother–son relationship, open, honest, affectionate and loving. We cuddle, kiss and tell each other 'I love you' numerous times throughout the day. James is keen on sport. He is musical, artistic, very bright and extremely popular. Whatever James wants to do, we have always encouraged and helped him – as with all parents, it's usually acting as a taxi driver. James will grow up to be a well-balanced, thoughtful, hard-working adult with a fantastic personality. I am proud to say that I have had some small part to play in that.

My only sadness since having James is that my Mother was not alive to see him. I had confided in her that I desperately wanted a baby. She told me I would make a wonderful mother and, philosophical as always, she said that if I was meant to have a child, it would happen. I am fully convinced that she got together with all the other angels in Heaven and answered my prayers to her, by sending James to me.

We had a wonderful relationship, very open, very honest, very affectionate, utter devotion and lots of laughs. I only hope that I will be as good a mother to James as my Mother was to me.

And all the while I was developing my business.

Not everyone would understand that this was a proper business for me, not only a labour of love. The RMS Disability Issues Consultancy delivers Disability Equality Training and other services to the private and public sector for both large and small organisations, at a competitive but reasonable rate. We have earned a good reputation and are highly respected. However, some people still have the impression that it might only be a hobby or something just to fill my time. Occasionally someone might contact me, for example, to speak to a group of midwives or a youth organisation or to give a lecture or presentation to a school. They set up a date and time and then say, as an afterthought, "Oh by the way, do you charge?" I don't charge charitable organisations, such as the Brownies or Rainbows, but, yes, those organisations that are earning money and charging for their services I do charge, and at the going rates. The money is not the main issue; the main issue is that I am passionate about it, and I believe things should be equal for disabled people.

I believe people need to be educated because unless they are made aware of the issues, they will not know how to go about making change. Although there is legislative backup now, there are still too many people with the ostrich syndrome of burying their heads in the sand and ignoring the true issues and barriers. They are the ones losing out on disabled customers and disabled employees with incredible skills that disabled people actually have. It's all about educating people.

Since 1995, in my time in business at RMS, I have helped to educate hundreds and thousands of people. If you consider that the average workshop I run can hold between 14 and 18 people and a university lecture or conference can attract between 20 and 300 people, over the years I think I can claim to have made quite an impact on the lives of many people. And that doesn't even take into account the strangers who stop me in the street to ask me questions or the interesting things people have learnt about me when observing, even staring, at me whilst I go about my daily activities!

# 20.

# On the Move Again

*Meeting Stuart Cable of the Stereophonics and Cerys Matthews of Catatonia as I celebrate my fortieth birthday.*

*And later in the bar, Tom Jones joins us for a chat.*

As 1997 rolled around, we felt that with our newly extended family, a bit more space was needed. Of course, our requirements were rather more difficult to satisfy than those of the average Mum, Dad and Son, so it took a while.

We viewed, among many others, a delightful bungalow in the suburb of Cardiff called Cyncoed. After a lot of agonizing over the matter, we finally settled on that one.

Our offer was accepted in March, and on 17 July we moved in. What a great day!

The bungalow had been chosen with the idea in mind that once we had made the alterations that we needed, it would be our home for life. This meant that it had to be able to accommodate not one but two people using electric wheelchairs, together with some separate accommodation for a live-in help, should it be required in the future. This was what had made the selection so difficult, but our chosen bungalow has an upper floor built into the eaves, which could be made into a self-contained apartment. Perfect.

Being us, there was no doubt that there would be a house-warming party, and, as it could be combined with James's second birthday, we made it a grand affair. And to cap it all, we all went to Disneyland in Paris in September.

My business was now getting some wider attention, and the following year I was nominated for the Welsh Woman of the Year Awards. I didn't win. The world was not yet ready for an empowered disabled woman, but the gala dinner was worth it!

Later that year James got his first taste of the limelight when he appeared as Joseph in the school nativity play. Unfortunately, he wound up as a single parent when Mary did a runner back to her mother, which must have given the producer a slight problem with the plot!

By now I was making some waves in the community with my advocacy for disabled people.

I have always had what my Mother called 'the gift of the gab', and whilst I am never rude, I can be incredibly assertive when I have to be. My desire to stick up for myself and for others as well started at a young age at the first school I attended for disabled people. I was pushing for a student representative body at the school so that if there were any issues, ideas or grievances the students wanted to address, they could be taken into account. Eventually when the new headmaster, Mr Crabb, arrived at the school, he thought this was a good idea and helped us to set up a student representative committee. Then at Florence Treloar School, I joined the debating team. We had quite a successful run and represented the school at County level. Also, although I did OK academically, I was not at the top of the class, but I did win the Ambassador for the School award, which was nice, although all it meant, actually, was that I had just behaved myself either out and about representing the school or when visitors came to the school. But having said that, I have always endeavoured to make people feel comfortable in my presence, and any slight reserve that anyone feels towards me usually disappears when they have spent a short time with me. I tend instinctively to find some way of breaking the ice.

Through the years, I got more and more political and by the time I got to Hereward College, I was part of the 'Disciplinary Committee' which also meant being holder of the key to the dorm or block, a position of enormous strategic and political significance. Anybody who had someone they wanted to sneak in would befriend the holder of the key. I never actually charged for this service but would arrange matters so that I couldn't see the entire transaction, discreetly holding the telescope in Nelson fashion, so to speak.

I was also voted vice president of the college student union, which gave me a chance to spend a weekend in Blackpool at the National Union of Students conference. It was quite an eye opener, a very enlightening experience because I learned, not just politics, but of other students who were not disabled, how they ticked and how to get up to the same things they were getting up to.

These activities got me noticed.

The BBC recruited me to do some hidden camera filming on the access situation for disabled people at the new Millennium Stadium in Cardiff for the Wales versus France rugby match. As it happens the access there is quite good, but given the population of disabled people in Wales compared to the actual number of accessible spaces provided at the stadium, the shortfall is huge.

I went to Sweden on a visit to the Centre for Excellence with United International Thalidomiders and then across the Atlantic to a conference in Canada on the re-licensing of Thalidomide. Whilst there I took the opportunity of interviewing Randy Warren, the then CEO of the Thalidomide Victims

Association of Canada (TVAC), who clearly had great concerns about the return of Thalidomide, but felt that it was better to be involved with the company rather than excluded. I further interviewed the CEO of Celgene, who obviously was keen to have Thalidomide re-licensed for more than just leprosy and to be able to have it re-licensed throughout Europe. Finally, I interviewed the very nervous doctor who had advocated Thalidomide for tumours, and he too was very keen for it to be re-licensed throughout Europe.

I came away with a very uneasy feeling and greatly concerned about the prospect of Thalidomide being re-licensed in the UK.

But in 2000, there was an important anniversary to be celebrated.

'Life begins at forty', so the old saying has it. Probably true for many, and the Biblical length of man's span, three score and ten, which I always felt must have been propounded by a young man, is also a yardstick for life.

But for Rosie and Stephen, it was significantly different.

Our fortieth birthdays fell within a few days of each other. We had often been told that no one knew what the survival rate would be for Thalidomide-impaired people. They (the so-called medical experts) did know that because of the abuse that our bodies have to endure – the way we have to do things being alien to the way the human skeleton and joints are used to doing things – that it would take its toll, but generally, in the medical profession, they were never able to say what the expected lifespan might be. Early reports were that Thalidomide-impaired people would not survive past their teens. Then, as a few passed that milestone, the estimate went to beyond the twenties and thirties. When we reached our thirties, we were told that we were thirty year-olds in seventy-year-old bodies! Realising we had reached our forties, but that technically, according to the pundits, we were eighty, it seemed like a good time to celebrate!

Our birthdays were eleven days apart, and we decided to have one great big bash. One good thing for sure is that when Stephen and Rosie give a party, people come because it is always done spectacularly, usually held at home, in a church hall or at an hotel with plenty food, drink and music. Our parties are all the more memorable because they bring together new and old friends: friends we have made through James and his school, sports or social activities; the oldest friends we have, some from our school and college days; my involvement in the disabled peoples movement; and friends from Steve's involvement in Lions International and, of course, work at his firm of solicitors. Not bad for a couple of pseudo-octogenarians.

On my actual birthday, Stephen decided to take me out for a romantic dinner, which, unbeknown to me, was to be a small party of our immediate family in a nice posh Cardiff hotel.

After dinner, we took our coffee into the bar so that I could have a cigarette. At the bar were the members of the group The Stereophonics. Much to my astonishment, I found that one of them, Stuart Cable, and I had a mutual friend, my old pal Keith 'Beefy' Jenkins who had died earlier that year.

Cerys Matthews was also there, and after a few more drinks, asked if she could have a ride on the back of my wheelchair – of course, I obliged. There was, I suppose, a chance that I might have become the first person to be charged with being drunk in charge of a wheelchair as we circled the bar in a state. The looks on the faces of my family were hysterical, and Cerys's family were equally amused.

A little while later, Tom Jones came into the bar! I went over to thank him for his generosity to me as a child. He had donated a little car to me, much like a bumper car at the carnival. When you sat on the seat, there was a sensor that made the car go. I still have the autographed picture and a plaque showing that he had donated it to me. I went over to say thanks, and he was very kind and gracious, pretending, quite convincingly, to remember who I was. We posed for photographs together to round off a memorable night.

Stephen couldn't have planned it better.

# 21.

# The European Year of Disabled People and Beyond

*3 December 2002, Rosie with Rhodri Morgan,*
*First Minister of National Assembly for Wales, and*
*Paul Murphy, Secretary of State for Wales.*

The year leading up to the 2003 European Year of Disabled People was, to say the least, going to be hectic, which seems to be an enjoyable pattern of my life.

I was honoured to have been asked by the Welsh Assembly Government to join with them, the Disability Rights Commission and Disability Wales (an all-Wales disability rights organisation) in helping stage five conferences in Wales titled 'Barriers Coming Down'. The conferences were in the form a rolling programme of events around Wales during July 2002. The conferences were primarily aimed at small businesses and local authorities, with particular emphasis on tourism. The point was to inform the delegates of their rights and obligations under the Disability Discrimination Act 1995, which at the time was entering one of its final stages of implementation, where service providers have to remove physical barriers that might prevent a disabled person from accessing the goods and services on offer. My presentation was to cover the History of Disabled People, the Definitions of Impairment and Disability, the difference between the Medical Model of Disability and the Social Model of Disability, rounding off with Disability Etiquette and time for questions!

The logistics of organising all of this were incredible. I obviously had to sort out child care for James, rearrange my PAs hours, try to find accessible accommodation around Wales, organise my transport to get to and from these events and condense my disability equality presentation – which generally would last at least four hours – into one and one–half hours!

The conferences were a great success, and I thoroughly enjoyed working alongside the other experts in their fields.

After the conferences had concluded, and looking forward to a quiet summer – which was not to be – I was approached by an old friend who was a governor at a local school for disabled children. The board of governors were looking for a person to sit as a governor with particular knowledge of disability issues. A quick phone call to the head teacher uncovered an amazing coincidence. The incumbent head was none other that Doug Dwyer, who had previously taught me and Beverley at Ysgol Erw'r Delyn. The deed was done, and I had yet another string to my bow.

I take my governor responsibilities very seriously, and although I am a huge advocate of disabled people having a right to attend mainstream school, I am also a firm believer in choice. All the children who attend Ty Gwyn School have learning difficulties at the severe end of the spectrum; on top of that, many of them have physical impairments. Further, many of the children who attend that school have life-limiting illnesses. Whilst I would love to see all of these children in mainstream schools, I regret to say that, certainly in Wales, if not also in the UK, we do not yet have the resources in place in mainstream schools to enable many of these children to attend.

In November I was asked to facilitate a workshop for Disability Wales at their annual conference. The title of the workshop was a little heavy, 'Mainstreaming Disability into Equal Opportunities Policies'. After a successful evening of entertainment filled with disability 'in' gags and jokes, I returned home to some sad news. My dear friend Janette (she of Hereward College days) had unexpectedly passed away. I was yet again devastated by sad news. Another of my soul-mates has been robbed of her ability to fulfil so many of her ambitions. Impairment-wise, Janette was similar to me in that we both had short legs, but whereas I have two fingers coming from each shoulder, Janette had nothing. On top of all that, a few years previously Janette had discovered that she also had diabetes. Janette's death was a great shock because although I knew that she was in hospital having had an operation for a hernia, when I had spoken to Janette's husband Bob, two days previously, everything had gone well, and Janette was as comfortable as could be expected. I understand that complications set in, which may have been Thalidomide related, and Janette's system just simply could not cope with the recovery process after this operation.

Just weeks before her death, she had appeared in a documentary celebrating the fortieth anniversary of Thalidomide-impaired people. One of the highlights of the documentary was Janette's fortieth birthday party filmed at a plush Cheshire hotel earlier in the year. Stephen, James and I had attended her party, at which she was the belle of the ball and, as always, an attentive hostess.

On the third of December every year, the International Day of Disabled People is celebrated. The turquoise-blue and baby-yellow ribbons that are worn on this day show our pride in and support for the disabled people's movement. The third of December 2002 was used to launch the 2003 round of celebrations to mark the European Year of Disabled People. In Wales it was celebrated by young disabled people taking over the Chamber at the Welsh National Assembly in Cardiff, and using the opportunity to ask Assembly Members lots of questions. On that very day, I had the honour of being invited to shadow Rhodri Morgan, our First Minister, at events both in Swansea and Cardiff. Unfortunately, his transport was not wheelchair accessible; therefore, he and his secretary had to travel in my car. It gave me a taste of what being a 'first lady' would be like. Travelling between venues, we had some quite interesting and frank discussions. The climax of the day was arriving at the National Assembly Buildings in Cardiff Bay, and prior to the youngsters question-and-answer sessions, I was allowed into the First Minister's inner sanctum, where Stephen and I met with the then Secretary of State for Wales Paul Murphy. This meeting allowed for Stephen to meet the MP for Torfaen, who in his previous life was a further education college lecturer and had taught British Constitution to a rowdy bunch of teenagers in the late 1970s, of which my husband was one. At the end of the day, I felt it was only right and proper to invite the First Minister to shadow me for a day. Regrettably, so far, he has not taken me up on this offer.

The most exciting thing for me, by far, however, was being involved in a documentary called *One in Six*, which was filmed for ITV1 in Wales to mark the significance of the year. There were five half-hour documentaries covering subjects such as disabled people in relationships, disabled people in art and disabled people and education. I was involved in the latter documentary on education. The uniqueness of this experience was that the producer Martin McCarthy encouraged us to put what we wanted into the documentaries, to be able to talk about subject matters that were important to us and to have as much input as we wanted in the way the final version of the documentary was portrayed. This was actually groundbreaking because lots of film producers and documentary makers come with their own agenda, and disabled people have not always had the opportunity of getting across the points that they want.

I am very proud of our documentary on education, particularly so because it won an award at the Celtic Film Festival for being the best educational documentary.

The next couple of years seemed to be a haze of working, socialising and fetching James to and from various sports and social activities. We met and have become good friends with some of the parents of other children at school with James. We regularly socialise and have meals out together. My nieces Jodie (of whom I am godmother) and Daisy are now young ladies and have recently been celebrating various milestones in their lives. However, they are not averse to an afternoon shopping or a night out at a concert with their old Auntie Rosie! My nephew Hugo, Debbie's youngest, is growing into a fine all-round sportsman.

On 26 November 2005, I nearly burst with pride as my 'baby' sang the Welsh National Anthem in front of 70,000 people at the Millennium Stadium, Cardiff, flanked by the Welsh rugby team. James had been chosen as the mascot for Wales in their game against Australia. Wales beat Australia for the first time in twenty years. By this time, James was himself a keen rugby player, and captained the Rhydypenau Primary School rugby team playing the position of hooker.

Into 2006 and another defining moment for me as James came to the end of his primary school education. James was awarded the Ian Asquith Prize at the presentation evening at his school. This award is given to a boy and girl from each year-six class for their contribution to school life and to recognise their personal qualities. It does not necessarily have to relate to academic achievement, but recognises important other skills learnt through school, and this is what Mr Nick Lewis (James's year-six teacher) had to say about James:

"This boy has a great sense of humour and is always enthusiastic during class. While working in groups, he is both active and supportive of his peers. There have been several occasions in the year when he has demonstrated his caring nature, putting others first and acting as a negotiator when there are disagreements between other members of the class. Academically he shows determination to constantly improve and develop as a learner, showing the qualities of resilience and resourcefulness. He is musically talented and has obvious rhythm. He is a keen sportsperson and has been active in after-school clubs. He has represented the school in football, cricket and rugby. His leadership qualities have been demonstrated through being captain of the school rugby team. The boy chosen this year for 6L is James Moriarty-Simmonds."

How proud a mum am I?

Now at Cardiff High School and enjoying new challenges, James also plays rugby for the junior teams with St Peter's RFC in Cardiff. One of his many aspirations is to play for Wales. Who knows what the future may hold?

Shortly after the New Year of 2006, I received a phone call asking me to contribute to a compilation of stories about women who have had disabled children, or disabled women who have had children; for a book called *Defiant Birth: Women Who Resist Medical Eugenics* by Melinda Tankard Reist. Mission accomplished. When the book was launched in London at the Palace of Westminster, I proudly read out some excerpts from my story.

Writing my story for that book made me realise that I *was* capable of writing my autobiography. This is a task I had started many years ago, and vowed every New Years Eve to complete. And as time was passing me by quickly, I should really get my act together.

So, for the past twelve months – apart from running my business; appearing as a regular guest on BBC radio Wales programmes; and being involved in two television documentaries, one for ITV1 Wales called *My Way* and, just to redress the balance, one for BBC1 Wales titled *Under The Doctor* as an expert on Thalidomide – I have been diligently spending every spare minute writing this book. Well actually, I haven't written it! In reality I have been talking it. I use voice-activated software on my computer which enables me to talk to my computer, and it types what

I say. That's technology for you, and what a difference technology has made to my life over the years!

However, back to 2006 and the absolute highlight of the year: our trip to America. It had been two years in the planning, very much like a military operation. We made a rather adventurous decision to spend time at two destinations, New York and Disney World, Florida. I use an electric wheelchair permanently; Steve uses an electric wheelchair whenever we go out and about and James, who was ten years old when we left for our holidays and celebrated his eleventh birthday whilst we were out there, gets about by conventional means. Apart from deciding on what sightseeing and touristy things we were going to do, we also had to think about more mundane things that the average family does not. For example, contact addresses for the local electric wheelchair repair firm, just in case either of our chairs needed attention, and contact addresses for the local limb-fitting centre, just in case Steve's artificial limbs needed repairing. We also had to organise the hiring of an adapted wheelchair-accessible car for a couple of sightseeing days in Florida.

Whilst we could not find a wheelchair-accessible taxi in New York for love nor money, every single bus was wheelchair accessible. When the bus drivers pulled up and saw us, they allowed passengers to disembark but prevented any other passengers from getting on the bus until they had us safely strapped in place after having accessed the bus either by ramp or lift. Also, as long as the subway could be accessed by a lift, one can get to most parts of New York. We actually took the subway to the Bronx so that James could fulfil one of his wish list items: seeing the New York Yankees play baseball at the Yankee Stadium. In this manner we pretty much 'did New York'.

Having had some great fun during our three weeks in America, one of the most profound moments for the three of us was driving along the Freeway 520, which took us to the Kennedy Space Center. The road passes through some quite barren landscape which is littered with carcasses of animals decimated by the resident vultures. As we passed from mainland Florida and onto the bridge that joins Merritt Island Nature Reserve to the mainland, the sense of history was immense. This was a road along which history-making Astronauts may have travelled on their journey to and from space, that unknown frontier which holds so much fascination for so many people.

# 22.

# The Drug That Keeps Bouncing Back

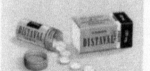

*Thalidomide/Distaval advertising – Safe and effective!*

I have been studying the advantages and drawbacks of Thalidomide since 1984 when I wrote my first paper on the subject whilst at University. The title was 'Thalidomide - the Drug, the Victims, the Unscrupulous Behaviour of the Distillers Company, and the Shortcomings of our Legal System'. There have been a number of papers and articles since then to my name and of course now this book. I have always tried to maintain a balanced view on the subject and have tried to understand why the medical profession and their patients have continued to promote the use of Thalidomide.

However, I have to admit that whilst gathering together all of the information I have, I now struggle to keep a balanced view.

It has been estimated that 50,000 babies were affected worldwide by the drug. Approximately 10 per cent of these babies survived with major disfiguring birth defects. Although the range of effects on the foetuses and babies varied from stillbirth to brain damage, through to massive internal damage, the most common adverse effect was Phocomelia (from the Greek *phoke,* 'seal' and *melos,* 'limb'), meaning 'deformities to the extremities,' or 'truncated arms and legs'. Some babies had little more than a head and trunk and tiny feet with seven or eight toes attached to the hips. There is a distinct window of time in early pregnancy during which Thalidomide strikes so devastatingly and that is thirty-four to fifty days after the last menstrual period. This is when limbs and ears 'bud' from the developing foetus and begin to grow. Thalidomide is so toxic in the uterus that many women miscarried.

The estimated number of Thalidomide-impaired adults surviving globally in 2008 was as follows:

| | | |
|---|---|---|
| United Kingdom | - | 450 |
| Germany/Holland/ | - | 2900 |
| Belgium | | |
| Japan | - | 300 |
| Brazil | - | 800 |
| (With some estimates suggesting even more) | | |
| Sweden | - | 110 |
| Canada | - | 110 |

In Spain and Italy, it is estimated that between two hundred and three hundred babies survived. There are estimated to be in excess of two hundred surviving adults scattered around the United States of America, the Caribbean Islands of Trinidad and Tobago, Norway and, closer to home, in Ireland.

Families affected by Thalidomide in this country genuinely believed, after the tragedy became public knowledge, that Thalidomide had been banned worldwide. However, the Royal Pharmaceutical Society has clarified that, "No drug is ever banned. It is withdrawn, and its licence taken away, but such drugs are still used for research purposes."

The Committee on Safety of Medicines has allowed Thalidomide to be used in the UK for research for the past thirty-eight years, and has permitted its use to increase.

So, now, perhaps, is a good time to tell you more about the key players in this story and to put my cards on the table on the drug that keeps bouncing back.

Before so doing, I would like to chart a Thalidomide Information and Timeline.

## 1954

When Thalidomide was discovered in Germany, the researchers were hoping to find an antibiotic or antihistamine. It was not to be, and so it became "A drug in search of a disease." In the process limited tests were undertaken, and, as we now know, it was never tested on pregnant animals. Free samples were distributed throughout the world.

Ex-Nazi officer Dr Heinrich Mückter, formerly in charge of virus research in wartime Krakow, Poland, became responsible for Chemie Grünenthal's research program. Otto Ambros, one of Grünenthal's Directors in the early 1950s, was a chemist and a Director of IG Farben, a company which supplied gasoline and rubber for Hitler's war effort. The pharmaceutical departments of the IG Farben cartel used the victims of the concentration camps during human experiments, such as the testing of new and unknown vaccines and drugs. In the Auschwitz files, correspondence was discovered between the camp Commander and Bayer Leverkusen. Bayer was part of IG Farben, a conglomerate of German chemical and pharmaceutical industries which formed the financial core of the Nazi regime. The correspondence dealt with the sale of one hundred and fifty female prisoners for experimental purposes, "...With a view to the planned experiments with a new sleep-inducing drug we would appreciate it if you could place a number of prisoners at our disposal (...)." Otto Ambros was responsible for the choice of location, planning, building and running of IG Farben, Auschwitz.

As operations manager at Auschwitz, he viewed inmates at the camp as a plentiful source of cheap labour. At the Nuremburg war trials, Ambrose was convicted of slavery and mass murder and sentenced to eight years in prison. Even whilst on trial, he was a target for United States recruiters from Project Paperclip. Project Paperclip was a post-war and Cold War operation carried out by the Joint Intelligence Objectives Agency. Paperclip had two aims, which were to exploit German scientists for American research and to then deny these intellectual resources to the Soviet Union. At least 1,600 scientists and their dependents were recruited and brought to the United States by Paperclip.

Ambrose had his prison sentence commuted by American officials after only three years.

## 1956/57

Thalidomide became widely available in Germany, even over the counter in chemists' shops. Within months as a result of mass marketing and advertising by Chemie Grünenthal, Thalidomide was available in numerous countries under several different brand names.

## 1958

In the United Kingdom Distillers Company (Biochemicals) Limited, the British manufacturers and licensees of Thalidomide, commenced marketing and distribution on a massive scale.

# 1959

In Germany, as early as mid-1959, the first reports of side effects – in the form of Peripheral Neuropathy in patients became apparent, as a result of the prolonged use of Thalidomide – began filtering through to Chemie Grünenthal. Peripheral Neuropathy becomes noticeable in damage to the nervous system. Ignoring these reports, Chemie Grünenthal denied them and continued to actively market the drug.

# 1961

In May of this year in America, Dr Francis Kelsey, newly appointed to the U.S. Food and Drug Administration, was unconvinced by the data which was being provided. As a result Dr Kelsey refused to allow Thalidomide to be distributed or marketed in the United States, except for clinical trials.

In November in Germany, Dr Widukind Lenz, almost simultaneously with Dr William McBride in Australia, made the association between babies being born with certain deformities (impairments) and their mothers having taken Thalidomide. Dr Lenz wrote to the companies asking them to withdraw the drug. They were most reluctant to do so and hoped to satisfy the Health Authorities by merely inserting the words 'not to be taken during pregnancy' on the label.

However, on 27 November 1961, Chemie Grünenthal reluctantly withdrew Thalidomide from the market. The epidemic of Thalidomide-impaired babies being born followed the sales figures of Thalidomide about eight months later. So as was to be expected, after withdrawal in Germany by the end of November 1961, an abrupt end to the malformation epidemic occurred by the end of July 1962.

On 2 December 1961, Distillers reluctantly withdrew Thalidomide from the British market. This took place four days before my first birthday. Again following the sales figures of Thalidomide, about eight months later in August 1962, there was an abrupt end to the epidemic of babies born with impairments caused by the drug. However, children with impairments accepted as attributable to Thalidomide (though not necessarily with documentary evidence of prescription) continued to be born until May 1963. This was because many people still had tablets containing Thalidomide in their homes, and either did not hear promptly of its dangers, or did not realise that the tablets contained Thalidomide.

Both Chemie Grünenthal and Distillers claimed that they had been forced to withdraw the drug, not because there was a chance that Thalidomide could cause foetal damage, but because press reports had undermined the basis of scientific discussion.

## 1962

In Belgium, Brazil, Canada, Italy and Japan, Thalidomide continued to be sold for several months after its withdrawal from the West German and British markets.

## 1963

Following the meeting in London of the initial sixty-two families, the parents were advised to issue writs alleging negligence and claiming damages against Distillers.

It was imperative that the parents acted immediately before the actions became statute-barred. Writs had to be issued within three years of the alleged injury, and in the case of Thalidomide-damaged babies, that meant within three years of conception. The writs were issued and filed in February 1963, and the applications for legal aid were eventually granted and certificates issued in June 1963. These were not full legal aid certificates, but provided sufficient legal aid assistance to keep the actions alive until the first case was finally settled.

## 1964

In Jerusalem Dr Jacob Sheskin, a medical doctor and Lithuanian Jew, used Thalidomide to provide some relief for a patient with leprosy. He found an old bottle of Thalidomide in his medicine cabinet, and thought that the drug would act as a sedative and help the patient to sleep. Apparently, some side effects of using the sedative became noticeable. Within three days some of the skin lesions healed. When the patient stopped taking Thalidomide the leprosy returned. It seemed that the drug acted as a suppressor, throwing the disease into retreat, although it could not actually eradicate the illness entirely from the patient. It is now well known that Thalidomide does not heal leprosy, but merely alleviates some of the side effects that patients experience as a result of taking other medication to eradicate their leprosy. After this discovery, Sheskin contacted Dr Heinrich Mückter to obtain further supplies of Thalidomide for a larger study programme.

It seems ironic that Dr Sheskin had to seek out the former Nazi military researcher at Chemie Grünenthal to help support his further research.

In this respect I ask myself, 'Why, given by now the notoriety of the drug, did Dr Sheskin still have supplies of Thalidomide in his cupboard when it was supposed to have been withdrawn some years before in Britain and Germany, and was allegedly only available in Israel for a few weeks in any event?'

Further, given the religious standing of Dr Sheskin, 'Why would Heinrich Mückter willingly give samples of Thalidomide to such a person?' My only possible conclusion is that Mückter realised that there might still be a use for Thalidomide, and if samples of the drug were distributed to doctors for research purposes, this would assist Chemie Grünenthal in two ways. Firstly, it would be a way of using up their stockpiles of Thalidomide; and secondly, if these researchers could keep finding ways and reasons for using the drug, then money, vast sums of money, could be made from it.

## 1967

Kimber Bull, a firm of London solicitors, was engaged to act collectively for the parents. On 20 December 1967, a pivotal meeting in the Thalidomide-litigation saga took place. There were two huge issues to consider. Initially, there was the difficulty of securing a judgement on a claim for damages for an unborn child for which there was no legal precedent. Secondly, the problem was establishing that Distillers were negligent in the testing and marketing of Thalidomide. Desmond Ackner, QC, the barrister engaged to act for the families, had to advise on these two issues. On the first issue, he estimated an 80 per cent chance of success, but on the odds of winning the second issue, he advised these were well below 50 per cent. On the strength of the company's position in relation to the second issue, someone at the meeting produced the magical 40 per cent compromise, being a settlement based on Distillers paying 40 per cent of any overall figure of compensation agreed. Ackner advised acceptance of the proposal. Distillers went further and insisted that the 40 per cent settlement would be agreed to only if every parent signed. This went hand in hand with the parents' abandoning all claims of negligence against the company. Our parents were effectively blackmailed into accepting the situation because legal aid would have been withdrawn, thus preventing them from continuing their proceedings. In addition, the added pressure brought by other parents, were all not to have agreed, would have been too much for any single set of parents to bear.

## 1968

In October other British parents were given leave to issue writs 'out of time'. The British, Canadian, Japanese and Swedish Thalidomide children received similar compensation following litigation to those in Germany. There are still a number of countries in which there appears to be no resolution of the compensation issue, notably Spain, Austria and Italy.

Japan was the only country in which both the Ministry of Health and Dai Nippon, the supplying company, agreed that Thalidomide was the cause of the epidemic of children being born with impairments caused by the drug. As a result the amount of compensation paid to the Japanese Thalidomide children was considerably higher than the amounts awarded in other countries.

In Germany eight prominent members of Chemie Grünenthal were, by now, being tried in criminal proceedings. The preliminary hearings lasted three years; the final proceedings, for a further two. The Grünenthal defence was conducted by the most expensive and garrulous lawyers in Germany, ably assisted by Chemie Grünenthal's permanent public relations unit. Every trick of the trade, and many more besides, was used by the defence lawyers to damage the prosecution case. Respected scientists and physicians were vilified, objections were raised ad nauseam, and the public prosecutor was officially challenged for bias. With its back to the wall, Chemie Grünenthal played its last card. The company warned that if the case continued, compensation for the Thalidomide families would have to wait for several years.

In Britain, the Medicines Act was passed by Parliament. Its purpose was to bring together most of the previous legislation on medicines. It introduced a number of other legal provisions for the control of medicines, and aimed to ensure the safety of pharmaceutical products in the United Kingdom.

## 1970

More than two years after the commencement of the criminal litigation in Germany, an agreement on compensation was reached. Compensation was paid to the German families, and, under a legal technicality, the proceedings against the Grünenthal representatives were abandoned. However, in their summing up, the judges stated that "Causal connection," had been established between the taking of Thalidomide and the malformations of babies.

## 1973–4

During this period the remaining British cases were settled along the same lines as the original sixty-two. Distillers further agreed to pay money into a trust fund which was to augment the individual settlements. It was for this purpose that the Thalidomide Trust was created. The Thalidomide Children's Trust was established on 10 August 1973, with the object of providing support to those people who had impairments caused by the drug Thalidomide, and began operation in 1974.

However, as part of the settlement process, families had to jump through hoops of fire. Each mother had to prove that she had taken the drug Thalidomide. The evidence to support this may have included having a dated prescription for Thalidomide; a doctor's statement, preferably a sworn affidavit, that he issued such a prescription at such a time, but kept no record of it; a mother's statement, preferably sworn, that she took Thalidomide at the relevant time, with an indication of its source; and a mother's ability to identify the tablet she took when shown a selection of tablets.

Unfortunately, some parents of Thalidomide children were unable to prove that their children were disabled as a result of the drug. Some because doctors were afraid of being held responsible for the injuries and actually destroyed records and prescriptions. Others because families changed doctors and any records of the mothers having been given Thalidomide were long since lost. Some families were unable to prove a relationship between the child's impairments and the drug for reasons of migration or a lack of willingness to admit that they had taken medication whilst pregnant. Then, of course, there were other cases where the father had actually been prescribed the medication and the mother helped herself to the tablets from the family medicine cabinet.

As children, we were paraded in our underwear in front of panels of doctors and so-called experts. We were required to perform 'tricks', such as attempting to walk, showing what could or could not be done physically and answering confusing and sometimes leading questions. This assessment, taken together with available medical records, was designed to assist the panel in coming to a decision as to which financial category the child would fit into when deciding on the level of compensation payable.

## 1990

In a television documentary, I was quoted as saying, "In about sixty years time, Thalidomide People will be extinct. We will go down in the history books as a generation of people that would, or at least should, never appear again. We are just a blip in the history of mankind."

## 1993

How wrong I was. News of the worst possible nightmare began to emerge from South America. The reintroduction of Thalidomide and the increase in its use worldwide for some diseases such as Myeloma, AIDS and Hansen's disease had increased the susceptibility of creating new victims. This happened, most disastrously, in Brazil where Thalidomide was introduced without regulation. Doctors were ill-advised, and those who were informed did not advise their female patients taking Thalidomide of the risks. Consequently, 120 children, a whole new generation of Thalidomide victims, were born. These children would face the same struggles which had beset the first generation, but with the additional burdens of their geographical locations and limited financial resources. In some cases these children were born into a life of poverty in the Amazon jungle.

## 1998

In the United States, the Celgene Corporation was given a licence on 16 July 1998 by the U.S. Food and Drug Administration to use Thalidomide only for the treatment of Erythema Nodosum Leprosum, a severe and debilitating condition associated with leprosy. However, as I suspected, a domino effect has taken place. Thalidomide has been and is now being used for a wide range of conditions and diseases throughout North America.

Thanks largely to the vigilance of the Thalidomide Victims Association of Canada (TVAC) and their collaboration with Celgene, a Thalidomide-distribution system called STEPS was devised. STEPS stand for

System for Thalidomide Education and Prescribing Safety. The STEPS programme requires that, before a patient is given Thalidomide, he or she must be thoroughly counselled about the danger of birth defects. The patient must watch a videotape of a 'Thalidomide victim' talking about the importance of avoiding pregnancy while taking the drug. Women must undergo pregnancy testing before, during and after treatment. Male patients must use two forms of barrier birth control.

## 1999

In December of this year, I had the good fortune to attend a TVAC conference in Canada dedicated to the whole subject of the re-licensing of Thalidomide, the STEPS programme and of how one doctor was advocating the use of Thalidomide for patients with brain tumours.

I met and interviewed Randy Warren, whose mother had also taken Thalidomide, who was at that time the Chief Executive Officer of TVAC. Randy clearly had great concerns about the return of Thalidomide but felt it better to work with Celgene rather than against them. I also spoke with John W. Jackson, Chairman of the Board and Chief Executive Officer at Celgene, who was obviously keen to have Thalidomide re-licensed for more than just leprosy, and to extend their operations and re-licensing objectives throughout Europe.

## 2001

In November of this year, another American pharmaceutical giant, the Pharmion Corporation, acquired exclusive marketing and distribution rights to Thalidomide and the STEPS programme from Celgene and its European subsidiary Penn Pharmaceuticals. The programme required that only licensed, registered providers could prescribe the drug. Providers cannot prescribe Thalidomide unless they have had a written report of a negative pregnancy test. Following initiation of treatment, pregnancy tests are conducted weekly for the first month and then monthly in women with regular menstrual cycles or bimonthly in women with irregular cycles. Female patients have to acknowledge in writing their understanding of reproductive warnings.

The prescribing physician is responsible for educating patients about Thalidomide and the STEPS programme. After this education, patients are required to sign a multi-copy informed consent form, which confirms his or her understanding of the risks and benefits of treatment. Although pharmacists do not have a role in providing this patient education, the pharmacy has to register with the manufacturer to qualify as a dispensing location.

## 2006

As I predicted, more and more uses for Thalidomide were being found. In May 2006 Celgene was granted accelerated approval by the U.S. Food and Drug Administration for the use of Thalomid(R) (thalidomide) in combination with Dexamethasone for the treatment of newly diagnosed Multiple Myeloma.

## 2007

On 1st March, the European Medicines Agency (EMEA) accepted for review Pharmion's marketing authorization application to use Thalidomide Pharmion(R) for untreated Multiple Myeloma. If approved, it would entitle the company to exclusively market the drug for ten years for the approved indications. Thalidomide Pharmion(R) must be prescribed and dispensed through the Pharmion Risk Management programme.

What of the other major players in this story?

## The British Government

Aside from Lord Ashley of Stoke, the former Labour MP who campaigned by raising the subject of Thalidomide and its surrounding issues periodically in Parliament in the 1960s and 1970s, there has never been a public inquiry regarding Thalidomide and the effect of the drug on the children (now adults) and their families. Neither has there been an apology from Government for the oversights which caused the tragedy. Apart from the Medicines Act 1968 and the Congenital Disabilities (Civil Liability) Act 1976, both of which were enacted as a direct result of the Thalidomide scandal, there has been no real legislative action taken to avoid the recurrence of another Thalidomide tragedy. Successive Governments have made some payments into the Thalidomide Trust to offset tax liabilities, and in 2004 the status of payments made from the Trust became tax exempt. Aside from these small initiatives, little has been done to ease the harshness of the lives of those affected by the drug.

Some years ago when the British Thalidomide Society celebrated its fortieth anniversary, an approach was made to the Government and the Greater London Council seeking permission to mark this special anniversary of the Thalidomide Society and to recognise the achievements of the "Thalidomide Family," which encompasses those of the membership who were similarly impaired. It was also hoped to extend this recognition to those who were no longer with us; and in addition to our families and those family members who had also passed away.

It was hoped that suitable recognition could be placed at the Guildhall in the City of London, as this would have acknowledged the importance of the work of the late Lady Mary Hoare and others who were instrumental in providing support during the early years of this story. It would further have recognised the contribution many Thalidomide-impaired people in the United Kingdom had made to society and the cause of disabled people generally.

Regrettably, a negative response was received to this request.

Interestingly, one wonders how differently things might have been had either Prince Andrew or Viscount Lindley, born in 1960 and 1961 respectively, been damaged by the drug. Would the groundswell of support that accompanied the tragedy in the 1960s have been greater with perhaps a different resolution had Queen Elizabeth II or Princess Margaret given birth to a child with Thalidomide deformities? In this respect we will never know.

# Distillers Company (Biochemicals) Limited

The company was formed on 31st March 1953 and is currently noted as being a non-trading company. However, its roots can be traced back to Liverpool and the Second World War. The Distillers Company, who made whisky and gin, were approached by the Government of the day to work on the production of larger quantities of penicillin. The Government recognised the significant benefits of treating infections by penicillin, but to do this required knowledge of the deep fermentation process and, of course, the only people with such experience were those in the brewing industry.

Distillers were asked to take on the project, and, as they already had a factory in Liverpool, they decided to locate their new factory close to the first base. The factory was built and sponsored by the Ministry of Supply and run on behalf of the Government by Distillers. The factory was completed towards the end of the war, and the first batch of penicillin was produced on Christmas Eve 1945. After the war, Distillers established a new division, under the name of Distillers Company (Biochemicals) Limited, specialising in deep fermentation techniques and produced a series of antibiotics, such as Streptomycin, used to treat tuberculosis, and Erythromycin, primarily used to treat chest infections.

The Biochemicals branch of Distillers obtained market rights for Thalidomide throughout the British Empire and began distributing Thalidomide in April 1958. In 1986 Distillers were acquired by Guinness PLC, who under pressure from campaigning groups, made further payments into the Thalidomide Trust.

In 1997 Guinness PLC and Grand Metropolitan PLC merged, and Diageo PLC was formed. The company name is comprised from the Latin *dia*, 'day' and the Greek *geo*, 'world'. The company takes this to mean that "Every day, everywhere, people celebrate with our brands."

It is, with this in mind, perhaps hardly surprising that after a further round of campaigning from proactive Thalidomide-impaired people, the company agreed to pay around £6.5 million per annum to the Thalidomide Trust under a covenant payable to 2037.

## Chemie Grünenthal

Now simply named Grünenthal, Grünenthal GmbH describes itself as an independent research-based global pharmaceutical company, specialising in pain therapy, contraception and innovative formulations for established active substance.

With striking similarity to Distillers in Britain, in 1948 Grünenthal was the first German company to manufacture and market penicillin.

Grünenthal advocate that the major hallmark of their working environment is no red tape, flexibility and flat hierarchies with major latitude for formulating and expressing ideas. Perhaps that ethos appealed so much to Heinrich Mückter when he joined the company shortly after the end of the Second World War and the collapse of the Nazi regime.

## Penn Pharmaceuticals Limited

The company was originally founded in 1979 as a pharmacy business in the village of Penn in

Buckinghamshire and in 1986 moved to Tredegar in South Wales – ironically, not more than 30 miles from where this story started at the Glossop Maternity Hospital in Cardiff.

The company specialised in contract out-sourcing services for the pharmaceutical industry. It had no own-brand products, but offered formulation development, distribution, analysis and clinical trials packaging as well as contract manufacturing.

Distributing Thalidomide to pharmacies on a named-patient basis only, by the mid-1990s Penn reported that volume manufacture had increased, with production rising from 10,000 to 200,000 capsules per month because of a rekindled interest in the treatment.

The Penn group of companies was acquired by the Celgene Corporation in October 2004 for £67 million.

## The Celgene Corporation

Celgene is a multi-national integrated biopharmaceutical company, which was formed in 1986. The company is primarily engaged in the discovery, development and commercialisation of innovative therapies designed to treat cancer and immunological diseases. The company boasts that driving commercial success and profitability are marketed products, which amongst others include Thalomid (thalidomide).

Celgene are currently undertaking much research into developing so called "cousins" of Thalidomide, which may eradicate the current known side effects of the drug. However, even if successful, this could take many years before we see a safe Thalidomide drug, if indeed ever.

From its company literature, it is clear that the sale of drugs such as Thalidomide, are the keystone to financial strength through which the company seeks to propel the successful development of new products over the coming years.

For Celgene, Thalidomide sales in 2006 produced revenue of $433 million, compared to $387.8 million in 2005.

## The Pharmion Corporation

Pharmion is a global biotech company that is dedicated to identifying and developing products for global haematology and oncology markets. It was formed on 26 August 1999. The rights to Thalidomide and the STEPS programme were acquired from Celgene in 2001.

In addition to its pending application in Europe, Pharmion holds exclusive marketing and distribution rights from the Celgene Corporation for Thalidomide in markets outside of North America, Japan and certain other Asian countries. Between 2003 and 2006 Pharmion registered Thalidomide Pharmion(R) in Australia, New Zealand, Turkey, Israel, South Korea and Thailand for the treatment of Multiple Myeloma after the failure of standard therapies.

Interestingly, the World Health Organisation does not recommend the use of Thalidomide and the European Union decided in favour of re-licensing the drug.

Whatever the outcome of the European discussions, it cannot be over emphasised that any potential benefit of using Thalidomide must be balanced with its known toxicity. Experience has shown that it is virtually impossible to develop and implement a foolproof surveillance mechanism to deal with the incorrect use of Thalidomide.

## The Children

For the most part, my fellow players, on what can be best described as the opposing team, have enjoyed a childhood which lead relatively quietly into teenage years and then onto adulthood. Sadly, some did not survive for very long after birth. Some have found life hard and have had difficulty in accepting the effects of such a cruel twist of fate. A fair proportion of the children have gone on to secure well-placed jobs in many fields, such as media and television work, law, accountancy, medicine, education and social work, to name but a few. Some have achieved success in business, acquiring a reputation for fairness and being recognised for the hard work which they put into making their businesses successful.

As time has progressed, the lessons of the drug have become even harsher. Many of the survivors have sadly died. Some as a result of natural causes, others from a passing associated with the anguish of living with their Thalidomide impairments.

I have lost two of my closest Thalidomide friends – Beverley Rastin, my 'terrible twin', and Janette Cooke, my lifelong friend and roommate at Hereward College - as a result of illnesses which might have been avoided but for the sometimes unknown internal effects of Thalidomide on the body. Consequently, as a group, we have seen our fair share of children (our offspring) being left without parents.

The group has also not escaped the realities of an ever-rising divorce rate.

However, having taken into account everything that life has thrown at us, we strive, with just a little bit more effort than most, to live and enjoy an ordinary life.

So, now you have a clearer picture of Thalidomide, the drug that never really went away, and to this I now append my honest perspective on its future, which I hope you will understand:

It seems to me that the pharmaceutical companies involved in promoting Thalidomide are 'sexing-up' the drug to make it sound more appealing than it actually is.

I do not support the re-licensing of the drug, and I believe there is insufficient evidence regarding the usefulness of Thalidomide to justify such re-licensing. Research should be channelled into finding other drugs that would be able to do the job just as well, if not better, and without such high risks or side effects.

Thalidomide should be made available free of charge for research purposes only in the hope that one day this Jekyll-and-Hyde drug may actually be made safe. I am also cautiously content with the continuation of the named-patient use of Thalidomide, again for research purposes only.

Thalidomide should be a drug of last resort. It should only be used where all previous medication has failed. This should be allied to extremely careful monitoring, and the guidelines already in existence should be stringently followed.

Human nature being what it is, I would advocate that globally, the Licensing Authorities require any existing guidelines be tightened and closely monitored. Worldwide legislation in each licensing country should be passed imposing a statutory duty of care on physicians and pharmacists, so that patients (and any child born with Thalidomide impairments) may be assured of some redress as a result of injury whilst the drug is being used.

There must be effective risk communication for patients taking Thalidomide. For this to work, the packaging of the drug will need to include warning messages in clear and plain language of the likely side effects. It would also be sensible to have vivid and memorable images of Thalidomide damage in the precautionary notes which accompany the medication. This should show clearly what could happen if the patient uses the drug other than in accordance with the prescription and the usage guidelines, such as those found in the STEPS and Pharmion Risk Management Programmes.

It is not my place to oppose an individual's right to make an 'informed decision' to use Thalidomide. However, I would earnestly urge the utmost thought and caution before anyone exercises his or her right to act on the informed decision which he or she may make.

Everything is subject to human error. On that basis I really feel there is an accident out there waiting to happen, and that there will be a third generation of Thalidomide babies. Consequently, someone must be accountable for providing support (both physical and financial) should the unthinkable happen.

Manufacturers, suppliers and physicians would do well to ponder the legal and moral implications of the greater use of the drug and its oft-used selling phrase as a "wonder drug" which, when its Mr Hyde persona appears is really not so wonderful at all ... is it?

# 23.

# A Very Ordinary Household

*Me and my boys - an ordinary family
doing extraordinary things.*

A friend once remarked, "But Rosie, the most remarkable thing about you and your family is that you are so ordinary."

It sounds a sort of backhanded compliment, and I suppose it would be for most families, but in our case it would be hard to find a better description. For our lives differ little from the thousands of families who live, work and play out their existences together.

In our household there are three typical sorts of days: The first is a typical work-at-home day.

Stephen, our ever-reliable live-in alarm clock, has us all awake and himself and James up before 8.00 a.m. when my Personal Assistant comes in. She assists with my personal requirements and needs first, and then with the hairdressing, breakfast and such. I then go to my room to put on my makeup and prepare myself to face the world.

Meanwhile, my PA carries on doing the housework, ironing, rubbish removal and all those chores that are a bit difficult for us to manage. She usually stays with me from 8.00 a.m. to 12.00 mid-day. I get to my desk about 11.00 a.m., check the e-mails, and, if there is a workshop coming up, I check through to make sure my PowerPoint presentation is up to date and, ensuring that, if handouts will be necessary, they are all correct. My PA helps me correlate all this and put together the delegate information packs which participants receive.

I work until about 3.30 p.m. when James comes home from school. I look forward to his getting home to discuss the day and to assist him with any homework needs. If there is an after-school activity he participates in, such as rugby, swimming, just visiting friends or playing football or cricket in the back garden, I am always available, even if it is just to play referee!

Steve, being chief cook and bottle washer at home, or as he likes to be known as Managing Director of Home Affairs, makes the family tea, and, after that and the kitchen clear-up, we will sometimes have a little downtime and watch one of the evening soaps, like *Coronation Street* or *East Enders*, for about an hour or so if we are not going out for the evening.

A workshop day is a bit different and starts, far too early for me, at about 6.00 a.m. I am usually up and looking gorgeous, of course, and ready to leave the house about 8.30 a.m., depending on the workshop venue.

All presentations are done with PowerPoint, which is, as far as I'm concerned, the best thing ever invented because it allows me to keep everything as up-to-date as possible. This means that we have to tote along a projector, laptop and all the assorted bits and pieces. We have got a nifty little trolley that carts all this.

Everything, including me, wheelchair and all, roll neatly into our converted Chrysler and, with Stephen at the wheel, we're off.

All delegates at the end of the day go away with an information pack, including handouts that would have covered all of the presentations. The programme is generally structured but is flexible enough to allow it to be revamped according to the number of attendees and the question time needed. It is preferable to allow the delegates to ask as many questions as needed rather than to rush them in order to get to the next section of the course. The day usually finishes about 4.30 p.m.

At weekends my PA doesn't come until 9.30 a.m., so I get to have a bit of a lie in. Then it's up and dressed as usual, and sometimes I'm off out for a Saturday of shopping with James. James and I love retail therapy, but Stephen is not so keen. So he diligently drops us off and then comes back for the shopping – and us – before we round off the evening with a bottle of wine and a Chinese takeaway. Sometimes we will go to a museum, the cinema or a live show. All three of us really appreciate live music and entertainment.

Once in a while, we'll go out and paint the town, if not red, just a little rosé, or possibly, Rosie.

So you see, our lives differ little from that of most families.

However, in the early days when we were children and teenagers, the medical profession had very few expectations of the abilities and capabilities of Thalidomide-impaired people. This included uncertainty as to whether or not we would be able to have children.

When in later years many of us went on to do so, any negative responses tended to be more social or practical ones, rather than medical. The fact that there are now more children of Thalidomide-impaired parents, than there are Thalidomide-impaired people speaks for itself in many ways. It reinforces the fact that Thalidomide-impaired people have been the protagonists of the disabled people's movement.

We have bulldozed our way through many of the barriers that society puts in the way of disabled people. The majority of us, despite living with constant

217

pain and aching joints, just quietly get on with our lives without our impairments being the main issue. We have used our strengths to bring about many changes in legislation and social policy.

Generally, society has become more accepting of seeing disabled people as a direct result of the Thalidomide story. Until this event, the majority of disabled people were accommodated in institutions, hospitals and other establishments away from the public eye.

Horrific injuries, often caused by the ravages of the two World Wars, were perceived as being too distressing for public view. This changed when many of the parents of Thalidomide children refused to allow their children to be seen as objects of pity, and were proud to be seen with their children as a whole family unit.

I have in my lifetime experienced discrimination, and negative attitudes – usually from ignorant, ill-informed people who were probably totally oblivious to their behaviour or its consequences.

I cope with the bad things and experiences, because mostly I have good things and good experiences and good people around me. Generally, I have a bubbly, confident personality, which sees me through the bad things. With a sense of humour, you can usually turn a negative thing around to see the funny side of it, and if you can laugh at yourself and the situation in which you find yourself – then you have cracked it.

When people stare at me, I smile at them. If people are rude, ignorant or mean to me, I either challenge them or ignore them. If people are obviously discriminating towards me, and they are in breach of legislation or not even prepared to implement best practices, then I definitely confront them, point out the error and do my best to change their attitude or the situation.

I am fortunate to be confident, in control and to have my opinions valued. I have a wonderful husband, a fabulous son and a much-loved extended family.

And so, at the end of this current, and I think by far my most challenging project yet, I look out of my office window on a world which has changed so much since I launched my assault on life.

I then turn my thoughts to what I would like to do next. Having worked in various branches of the media, I would love to extend my previous ad hoc appearances to something more regular – perhaps as the first obviously disabled female newsreader on national television. Then my hope for true inclusion and acceptance would really be fulfilled. However, if all else fails, James says I have a great face for radio!

But, really, whatever I or my lovely family choose to do, I simply hope that we have strength for whatever that task may be and, indeed, whatever is in hand that we have time to do all of the things that we have planned. And above all, that laughter and sunshine be with us everyday.

It would have been unimaginable over forty years ago to think that I would one day sit and look back on a catalogue of events that started in Germany, hundreds of miles away from where I was conceived, a chain of events that my beloved parents had no control over that would ultimately leave me with four fingers and thirteen toes, of which I am rightly and justifiably proud.

*James as Mascot, with the late Ray Gravell (Rugby legend and broadcaster) Wales v. Australia Rugby match on 26 November 2005 Millennium Stadium, Cardiff.*

*J*ust an ordinary boisterous boy,

*A*lways ready to help, not annoy,

*M*y pride, my joy, one of two loves in my life,

*E*ndearing, charming, – my haven from trouble and strife,

*S*porty, mischievous, naughty and nice! A God-given gift and gemstone of life

# Epilogue

Since publication of the first edition of this book, the response from my Thalidomide-impaired peers and others has been overwhelming. There have been some interesting developments in connection with the use of Thalidomide, and, on a personal note, I have achieved some of the aims that I outlined in Chapter 23.

To bring my story right up to date, it would be amiss of me not to detail the changes that have taken place regarding the ongoing use of Thalidomide and its current 'licensed status,' as well as outlining some of my personal achievements since publication. I also want to mention some of the people who have made contact with me from my past, in some instances my very distant past – even back to the very day I was born.

The latter part of 2007 came and went in a whirl of newspaper and magazine interviews for UK publications and radio interviews as far away as Spain. This allowed me to reach an audience for my story that might not otherwise have been possible to target. As a result I renewed friendships with old school and college friends that had long passed into the dusty vaults of the memory. Members of my extended family from locations as diverse as London and Sheffield happened by chance to hear of the book. I am now in regular contact with relatives from both my Mum and Dad's side of the family, some of who I had not been in contact with since my Mum's funeral.

I have been deeply humbled by the messages of goodwill and congratulations that followed publication.

As well as the goodwill messages from friends and family, I was particularly pleased to hear from Moreen Standing, a member of staff from my days at Florence Treloar School. She acquired a copy of the book after a feature in the *Daily Mail*, and we now exchange regular e-mail correspondence, sometimes of a fun nature and sometimes reminiscing about life in Treloar's. This renewed acquaintance has allowed me to catch up with news of some of the teachers who were instrumental in helping my education and to find out how life after my time with them has worked out.

However, of all the letters and messages, the most astonishing was a letter which arrived from a lady by the name of Valerie Jones. With a surname like Jones, it was a safe bet that the letter was from a person of Welsh origin, but I could never have dreamed of the significance that such a letter would hold. By chance Valerie had tuned in to listen to BBC Radio 4's *Woman's Hour* that was running a feature broadcast on 30 June 2008 concerning the availability of Thalidomide. On hearing the Moriarty portion of my surname, she realised in an instant that she had played a significant part in bringing me into the world. As a young student doctor in 1960 undertaking her obstetrics training, Valerie was assigned to help my Mum during labour and my subsequent birth. In her letter Valerie describes remembering, "Her [my Mum] clearly – so young and brave with reddish brown hair and freckles." She went on to describe how my Mum had told her that she was going to give me an especially pretty name, "Rosaleen", which she has never forgotten. By a further irony, Valerie (now

223

a retired GP) lives close to the Nuffield Orthopaedic Centre where I spent so much time having operations and treatment.

The letter was in some ways strangely eerie, as apart from my Mum, who had limited recollection of my arrival, as she was preoccupied with giving birth to me and was then immediately sedated, I was now reading a letter from someone who had actually delivered me. Even more surprising was that my birth was the first time Valerie had delivered a baby.

I was thrilled and delighted to receive Valerie's letter, not least because it gave me an opportunity to find out more about the circumstances of my birth and the trauma that it caused in the hospital, and I resolved to speak with her to try and fill in the gaps.

For various reasons, not least work commitments, I did not get around to speaking with Valerie for a number of weeks after her letter arrived. It was, therefore, with some trepidation that on a bright autumn afternoon, but a few days after what would have been my beloved Mother's sixty-sixth birthday, I telephoned and spoke for the first time to the person who first held me and for whom those moments in 1960 after my birth had a profound effect on her early medical training.

What she had to say was so enlightening, but as was to be expected, there was awkwardness during the first few sentences, rather like the stilted telephone conversation you have when you speak with a prospective new employer for the first time. However, after the initial introductions, it became clear that despite the passing of years the memory

224

of my birth had not dimmed. It seems that on the day I was born, life on the delivery ward of Glossop Maternity Hospital had been particularly traumatic. About twelve (sometimes difficult) deliveries had already taken place, and whilst I was pretty much to term, it had been decided to induce my delivery.

I knew my Mum had been poorly during her pregnancy, but I had no idea just how ill she was. Valerie was able to tell me that Mum was suffering from severe pre-eclamptic toxaemia, and there was real cause for concern for both mother and baby.

In attendance for my arrival into the world was Mr Edward Morris (the senior registrar), Valerie, her student doctor colleague and friend Diane, together with one other student, the theatre sister and a junior midwife. After the process of inducing had started, it became clear that my Mum had dilated sufficiently for the birth to proceed, and so my arrival began. As my head appeared from the birth canal, Valerie recalled that the umbilical cord was wrapped around my neck. But that was the least of the worries for the delivery staff on duty that cold December night.

Following the appearance of my head with a mop of black hair, and having had the umbilical cord removed from around my neck, came the final surge of delivery. Sister had told Valerie to catch hold of my shoulders and pull me out, and advised Mum to give one hard push. Valerie remembers trying to grip my shoulders but, puzzled, thought all she could feel were some fingers. At that moment Mum pushed, and apparently I almost wriggled out myself. Valerie recalled a, "deathly silence" as the enormity of my deformities became apparent. The deathly silence was eventually broken only by my roaring and screaming, and then Sister calmly and firmly took control.

Valerie's reaction was to say the least understandable: "God, what have I done?" Her worries and concerns were lightened only by the strength of my lungs, and I was able to tell her that those lungs still make as much noise today as they did in 1960!

Mum was apparently sedated because of a real threat of her having seizures as a result of her dangerously high blood pressure. Mum had always believed she was sedated for fear of her reaction to having a disabled child. Perhaps because of the shocked state of the staff and in all the mayhem, nobody thought to explain properly to Mum the reasons for her being sedated.

News of my birth soon travelled throughout the hospital, as a succession of senior doctors tried to establish, to no avail, exactly what had caused my lack of arms and legs, without having any real understanding of what had transpired.

In the typically stoic fashion of the medical profession, Valerie went on to complete her training and shortly thereafter left Cardiff. Having travelled the world using her medical skills, Valerie never came across another Thalidomide baby. She recalled fondly of periodically seeing me in media coverage over the years and wondering how I was and how my parents coped following my birth.

Our telephone conversation ended with a promise to meet when Valerie next comes to Cardiff to indulge another passion in her life, music and the Cardiff Singer of the World Competition.

It will be strange meeting the person who helped give life to the story found in the pages of this book, but as a great believer in fate, I am sure that Valerie's chance listening to *Woman's Hour* was meant to be and will allow the final piece of the jigsaw for those early days to be fitted into place.

As for Thalidomide itself, I have watched the recent developments on the re-licensing of the drug with intense interest.

In June 2007 the European Commission granted Celgene full marketing authorization for Revlimid(R), Thalidomide with other combinations.

On 24 January 2008, the European Medicines Agency (EMEA) announced that the Committee for Medicinal Products for Human Use adopted a positive opinion, recommending granting a marketing authorisation to Pharmion for Thalidomide Pharmion(R) to treat Multiple Myeloma, a rare cancer of the bone marrow. Re-licensing approval was granted.

Two months after the granting of the licence to Pharmion, on 7 March 2008, Celgene acquired Pharmion in a $2.9 billion transaction.

The transaction resulted in the combination of what Celgene described as, "Three medically meaningful therapies, Revlimide(R), Thalomid(R) and Vidaza(R), treating patients worldwide." Celgene expect the transaction to generate multiple global revenues by operating in nearly 100 countries over the next five years and beyond.

In combining the two companies, what Celgene have done is to create a global leader in haematology/ oncology. In addition, Celgene have indicated that they have a number of what they describe as, "Innovative programs encompassing therapies for immune/inflammatory disorders, haematological malignancies and other cancers."

Currently, 40 per cent of the drug used in the UK is Thalidomide Pharmion(R), and is now sold through Celgene at great cost. The remaining 60 per cent comes from other sources. Celgene advocate that their Thalidomide-related products are prescribed and used, only within the context of the Risk Management Programme. Apparently, the remaining 60 per cent is used outside of an established risk management programme, but presumably within government guidelines. Celgene would like to be the sole manufacture of the drug, and remove other sources of Thalidomide from the market in the UK. Some might say that this is commendable. However, I am concerned that this will create a worldwide monopoly on a highly lucrative but dangerous drug.

So, as I both feared and predicted, Thalidomide will be used for more and more conditions. Of course, as the additional use increases, the risk of more children born disabled because of the drug will also be greater.

A small crumb of comfort in this continued global onslaught, is that Celgene have acknowledged that they, "Will do the right thing" in the event of the unthinkable occurring with the birth of a Thalidomide-impaired baby as a result of a patient taking one of the their Thalidomide manufactured drugs.

However, the need for ongoing use of a Risk Management Programme – together with stringent, uniform and worldwide guidelines for patients using

Thalidomide – continues to weigh heavily on my mind. To this end I, and no doubt other interested parties, will continue to monitor the situation.

In my opinion whatever the outcome of European and worldwide usage, it cannot be over emphasised that any potential benefit of using Thalidomide must be balanced with its known toxicity. Experience has shown that it is virtually impossible to develop and implement a foolproof surveillance mechanism to deal with the incorrect use of Thalidomide.

Globally, concern over the continued use of Thalidomide also dominates the minds of Thalidomide-impaired people who, like those in the United Kingdom, are concerned about the effects of ageing as we move towards our fifth decade.

On 3 April 2008, Thalidomiders (as some like to be called) gathered en-masse outside the German Embassy in London to protest at the lack of commitment to greater financial and practical assistance by Chemie Grünenthal. I joined that demonstration of European solidarity wearing two hats. Firstly, as a Thalidomide-impaired person; secondly, in my capacity as a presenter for a radio documentary series on 'Thalidomide – fifty years on.' I interviewed leading figures in the ongoing campaign and gained an insight into the lives of those of our number who live in Austria, Spain and Italy, where little or no financial support is given to those citizens affected by the Thalidomide tragedy.

Shortly after the demonstration, I had an opportunity to speak with Lord Ashley, who was still as passionate about the problems facing Thalidomide-impaired people as he was in the 1970s. I also spoke with Lord Morris of Manchester, who, as Alf Morris MP, was the first Minister for Disabled People in 1974 in the Labour Government of Harold Wilson. Lord Morris explained how he and Lord Ashley were pivotal in steering the Thalidomide story through the parliamentary process and trying to keep it in the public eye. Speaking with Philip Knightley, a key member of the *Sunday Times* team under the editorship of Harold Evans, provided a unique insight into how committed the press were to helping the families. He gave a firsthand view of just how far the *Sunday Times* team were prepared to go in challenging the *sub judice* laws.

I then had the privilege of speaking with five Thalidomide-impaired people throughout Wales. Sue Kent, Julie George, Mark Hillier, Neal Merry and Andrew Paddison provided an intriguing insight as to how those, from very differing backgrounds, dealt with the challenges of living with their Thalidomide impairments. It was interesting to see just how my own belief, that most of us live an ordinary life, was very much transposed into the lives of these very real and wonderful personalities.

The upshot of this work was a two-part documentary aired during the early summer of 2008 on BBC Radio Wales. The series was received with positive reviews from many quarters, including senior members of the BBC Wales managerial structure.

As a result of the success of the Thalidomide programmes, some television work was offered to me by the production team at Telesgop Television, a media company based in Swansea. They invited me to be a guest presenter on one of the days of filming at the 2008 Royal Welsh Show held in Builth Wells, Mid Wales. This prestigious yearly event is a European showcase for all that is best about Welsh life. So, along with James, we toured the event as city slickers visiting the show for the very first time. I had the chance to sample some home-grown Welsh produce and view products made in Wales. James got to further his fledging television career as a novice in a canoe. It was an honour to be asked to host such a feature not only because the event attracts a huge television audience in Wales but also because I was lining up with Welsh celebrities from the world of pop music and with seasoned television presenters with many years of television presenting to their credit.

Aside from my media work, I continue to campaign for full inclusion for all disabled people and hope that in some small way my story will empower my disabled contemporaries to reach for the stars and conquer the universe.

My family continue to be my strength, and I am thankful that Stephen and James continue to support my work and help me to achieve the goals that I set myself.

The four fingers and thirteen toes with which I have been blessed are certainly feeling the effects of middle age, but still have a lot more energy in them. Who knows? In the future I may even have enough material to write a sequel to my story. Maybe, just to be sure I haven't lost any along the way, *Four Fingers and Thirteen Toes: Recounting the Digits* will be the title....

Watch this space!

9 781438 942995